Wild Workshop

Anne Carson is Professor of Classics at McGill University in Montreal. She is the author of *Plainwater; Glass, Irony and God*; and *Eros the Bittersweet: An Essay*, all published in the USA.

Kay Adshead is both a writer and an actress, and has played parts as diverse as Cathy in the BBC's *Wuthering Heights* and the female Mancunian wrestler Trafford Tanzi, in Claire Luckham's play of that name. Her own first play was *Thatcher's Women*. She is currently working on a corpus of performance poetry under the title *Strip-Search*.

Bridget Meeds was born in Syracuse, New York, and has degrees from both Ithaca College and Lancaster University. She has been an editor and an electric-bass guitarist, and now works as a secretary for scientists.

Wild Workshop

ANN CARSON, KAY ADSHEAD,
BRIDGET MEEDS

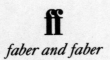

faber and faber

First published in 1997
by Faber and Faber Limited
3 Queen Square London WC1N 3AU

Photoset by Wilmaset Ltd, Wirral
Printed in England by Mackays of Chatham Plc, Chatham, Kent

Anne Carson, Kay Adshead and Bridget Meeds are hereby identified as
authors of this work in accordance with Section 77 of the Copyright,
Designs and Patents Act 1988

A CIP record for this book
is available from the British Library

ISBN 0-571-19107-X

2 4 6 8 10 9 7 5 3 1

Contents

ANNE CARSON *The Glass Essay*

I

I can hear little clicks inside my dream.
Night drips its silver tap
down the back.
At 4 a.m. I wake. Thinking

of the man who
left in September.
His name was Law.

My face in the bathroom mirror
has white streaks down it.
I rinse the face and return to bed.
Tomorrow I am going to visit my mother.

SHE

She lives on a moor in the north.
She lives alone.
Spring opens like a blade there.
I travel all day on trains and bring a lot of books –

some for my mother, some for me
including *The Collected Works of Emily Brontë*.
This is my favourite author.

Also my main fear, which I mean to confront.
Whenever I visit my mother
I feel I am turning into Emily Brontë,

my lonely life around me like a moor,
my ungainly body stumping over the mud flats with a look of
    transformation
that dies when I come in the kitchen door.
What meat is it, Emily, we need?

THREE

Three silent women at the kitchen table.
My mother's kitchen is dark and small but out the window
there is the moor, paralysed with ice.
It extends as far as the eye can see

over flat miles to a solid unlit white sky.
Mother and I are chewing lettuce carefully.
The kitchen wall clock emits a ragged low buzz that jumps

once a minute over the twelve.
I have Emily p. 216 propped open on the sugarbowl
but am covertly watching my mother.

A thousand questions hit my eyes from the inside.
My mother is studying her lettuce.
I turn to p. 217.

'In my flight through the kitchen I knocked over Hareton
who was hanging a litter of puppies
from a chairback in the doorway ... '

It is as if we have all been lowered into an atmosphere of glass.
Now and then a remark trails through the glass.
Taxes on the back lot. Not a good melon,

too early for melons.
Hairdresser in town found God, closes shop every Tuesday.
Mice in the teatowel drawer again.
Little pellets. Chew off

the corners of the napkins, if they knew
what paper napkins cost nowadays.
Rain tonight.

Rain tomorrow.
That volcano in the Philippines at it again. What's her name
Anderson died no not Shirley

the opera singer. Negress.
Cancer.
Not eating your garnish, you don't like pimento?

Out the window I can see dead leaves ticking over the flatland
and dregs of snow scarred by pine filth.
At the middle of the moor

where the ground goes down into a depression,
the ice has begun to unclench.
Black open water comes

curdling up like anger. My mother speaks suddenly.
That psychotherapy's not doing you much good is it?
You aren't getting over him.

My mother has a way of summing things up.
She never liked Law much
but she liked the idea of me having a man and getting on with
     life.

Well he's a taker and you're a giver I hope it works out,
was all she said after she met him.
Give and take were just words to me

at the time. I had not been in love before.
It was like a wheel rolling downhill.
But early this morning while mother slept

and I was downstairs reading the part in *Wuthering Heights*
where Heathcliff clings at the lattice in the storm sobbing
Come in! Come in! to the ghost of his heart's darling,

I fell on my knees on the rug and sobbed too.
She knows how to hang puppies,
that Emily.

It isn't like taking an aspirin you know, I answer feebly.
Dr Haw says grief is a long process.
She frowns. What does it accomplish

all that raking up the past?
Oh – I spread my hands –
I prevail! I look her in the eye.
She grins. Yes you do.

WHACHER

Whacher,
Emily's habitual spelling of this word,
has caused confusion.
For example

in the first line of the poem printed *Tell me, whether, is it*
   winter?
in the Shakespeare Head edition.
But whacher is what she wrote.

Whacher is what she was.
She whached God and humans and moor wind and open night.
She whached eyes, stars, inside, outside, actual weather.

She whached the bars of time, which broke.
She whached the poor core of the world,
wide open.

To be a whacher is not a choice.
There is nowhere to get away from it,
no ledge to climb up to – like a swimmer

who walks out of the water at sunset
shaking the drops off, it just flies open.
To be a whacher is not in itself sad or happy,

although she uses these words in her verse
as she uses the emotions of sexual union in her novel,
grazing with euphemism the work of whaching.

But it has no name.
It is transparent.
Sometimes she calls it Thou.

'Emily is in the parlour brushing the carpet,'
records Charlotte in 1828.
Unsociable even at home

and unable to meet the eyes of strangers when she ventured out,
Emily made her awkward way
across days and years whose bareness appals her biographers.

This sad stunted life, says one.
Uninteresting, unremarkable, wracked by disappointment
and despair, says another.

She could have been a great navigator if she'd been male,
suggests a third. Meanwhile
Emily continued to brush into the carpet the question,

Why cast the world away.
For someone hooked up to Thou,
the world may have seemed a kind of half-finished sentence.

But in between the neighbour who recalls her
coming in from a walk on the moors
with her face 'lit up by a divine light'

and the sister who tells us
Emily never made a friend in her life,
is a space where the little raw soul

slips through.
It goes skimming the deep keel like a storm petrel,
out of sight.

The little raw soul was caught by no one.
She didn't have friends, children, sex, religion, marriage,
    success, a salary
or a fear of death. She worked

in total six months of her life (at a school in Halifax)
and died on the sofa at home at 2 p.m. on a winter afternoon
in her thirty-first year. She spent

most of the hours of her life brushing the carpet,
walking the moor
or whaching. She says

it gave her peace.
'All tight and right in which condition it is to be hoped we shall
    all be this day 4 years,'
she wrote in her Diary Paper of 1837.

Yet her poetry from beginning to end is concerned with prisons,
vaults, cages, bars, curbs, bits, bolts, fetters,
locked windows, narrow frames, aching walls.

'Why all the fuss?' asks one critic.
'She wanted liberty. Well didn't she have it?
A reasonably satisfactory homelife,

a most satisfactory dreamlife – why all this beating of wings?
What was this cage, invisible to us,
which she felt herself to be confined in?'

Well there are many ways of being held prisoner,
I am thinking as I stride over the moor.
As a rule after lunch mother has a nap

and I go out to walk.
The bare blue trees and bleached wooden sky of April
carve into me with knives of light.

Something inside it reminds me of childhood –
it is the light of the stalled time after lunch
when clocks tick

and hearts shut
and fathers leave to go back to work
and mothers stand at the kitchen sink pondering

something they never tell.
You remember too much,
my mother said to me recently.

Why hold onto all that? And I said,
Where can I put it down?
She shifted to a question about airports.

Crops of ice are changing to mud all around me
as I push on across the moor
warmed by drifts from the pale blue sun.

On the edge of the moor our pines
dip and coast in breezes
from somewhere else.

Perhaps the hardest thing about losing a lover is
to watch the year repeat its days.
It is as if I could dip my hand down

into time and scoop up
blue and green lozenges of April heat
a year ago in another country.

I can feel that other day running underneath this one
like an old videotape – here we go fast around the last corner
up the hill to his house, shadows

of limes and roses blowing in the car window
and music spraying from the radio and him
singing and touching my left hand to his lips.

Law lived in a high blue room from which he could see the sea.
Time in its transparent loops as it passes beneath me now
still carries the sound of the telephone in that room

and traffic far off and doves under the window
chuckling coolly and his voice saying,
You beauty. I can feel that beauty's

heart beating inside mine as she presses into his arms in the high
     blue room –
No, I say aloud. I force my arms down
through air which is suddenly cold and heavy as water

and the videotape jerks to a halt
like a glass slide under a drop of blood.
I stop and turn and stand into the wind,

which now plunges towards me over the moor.
When Law left I felt so bad I thought I would die.
This is not uncommon.

I took up the practice of meditation.
Each morning I sat on the floor in front of my sofa
and chanted bits of old Latin prayers.

De profundis clamavi ad te Domine.
Each morning a vision came to me.
Gradually I understood that these were naked glimpses of my
     soul.

I called them Nudes.
Nude #1. Woman alone on a hill.
She stands into the wind.

It is a hard wind slanting from the north.
Long flaps and shreds of flesh rip off the woman's body and lift
and blow away on the wind, leaving

an exposed column of nerve and blood and muscle
calling mutely through lipless mouth.
It pains me to record this,

I am not a melodramatic person.
But soul is 'hewn in a wild workshop'
as Charlotte Brontë says of *Wuthering Heights*.

Charlotte's preface to *Wuthering Heights* is a publicist's
  masterpiece.
Like someone carefully not looking at a scorpion
crouched on the arm of the sofa Charlotte

talks firmly and calmly
about the other furniture of Emily's workshop – about
the inexorable spirit ('stronger than a man, simpler than a
  child'),

the cruel illness ('pain no words can render'),
the autonomous end ('she sank rapidly, she made haste to leave
  us')
and about Emily's total subjection

to a creative project she could neither understand nor control,
and for which she deserves no more praise nor blame
than if she had opened her mouth

'to breathe lightning'. The scorpion is inching down
the arm of the sofa while Charlotte
continues to speak helpfully about lightning

and other weather we may expect to experience
when we enter Emily's electrical atmosphere.
It is 'a horror of great darkness' that awaits us there

but Emily is not responsible. Emily was in the grip.
'Having formed these beings she did not know what she had
  done,'
says Charlotte (of Heathcliff and Earnshaw and Catherine).

Well there are many ways of being held prisoner.
The scorpion takes a light spring and lands on our left knee
as Charlotte concludes, 'On herself she had no pity.'

Pitiless too are the Heights, which Emily called Wuthering
because of their 'bracing ventilation'
and 'a north wind over the edge'.

Whaching a north wind grind the moor
that surrounded her father's house on every side,
formed of a kind of rock called millstone grit,

taught Emily all she knew about love and its necessities —
an angry education that shapes the way her characters
use one another. 'My love for Heathcliff,' says Catherine,

'resembles the eternal rocks beneath —
a source of little visible delight, but necessary.'
Necessary? I notice the sun has dimmed

and the afternoon air sharpening.
I turn and start to recross the moor towards home.
What are the imperatives

that hold people like Catherine and Heathcliff
together and apart, like pores blown into hot rock
and then stranded out of reach

of one another when it hardens? What kind of necessity is that?
The last time I saw Law was a black night in September.
Autumn had begun,

my knees were cold inside my clothes.
A chill fragment of moon rose.
He stood in my living room and spoke

without looking at me. Not enough spin on it,
he said of our five years of love.
Inside my chest I felt my heart snap into two pieces

which floated apart. By now I was so cold
it was like burning. I put out my hand
to touch his. He moved back.

I don't want to be sexual with you, he said. Everything gets
    crazy.
But now he was looking at me.
Yes, I said as I began to remove my clothes.

Everything gets crazy. When nude
I turned my back because he likes the back.
He moved onto me.

Everything I know about love and its necessities
I learned in that one moment
when I found myself

thrusting my little burning red backside like a baboon
at a man who no longer cherished me.
There was no area of my mind

not appalled by this action, no part of my body
that could have done otherwise.
But to talk of mind and body begs the question.

Soul is the place,
stretched like a surface of millstone grit between body and
    mind,
where such necessity grinds itself out.

Soul is what I kept watch on all that night.
Law stayed with me.
We lay on top of the covers as if it weren't really a night of sleep
    and time,

caressing and singing to one another in our made-up language
like the children we used to be.
That was a night that centred Heaven and Hell,

as Emily would say. We tried to fuck
but he remained limp, although happy. I came
again and again, each time accumulating lucidity,

until at last I was floating high up near the ceiling looking down
on the two souls clasped there on the bed
with their mortal boundaries

visible around them like lines on a map.
I saw the lines harden.
He left in the morning.

It is very cold
walking into the long scraped April wind.
At this time of year there is no sunset
just some movements inside the light and then a sinking away.

KITCHEN

Kitchen is quiet as a bone when I come in.
No sound from the rest of the house.
I wait a moment
then open the fridge.

Brilliant as a spaceship it exhales cold confusion.
My mother lives alone and eats little but her fridge is always
    crammed.
After extracting the yogurt container

from beneath a wily arrangement of leftover blocks of
    Christmas cake
wrapped in foil and prescription medicine bottles
I close the fridge door. Bluish dusk

fills the room like a sea slid back.
I lean against the sink.
White foods taste best to me

and I prefer to eat alone, I don't know why.
Once I heard girls singing a May Day song that went:

> Violante in the pantry
> Gnawing at a mutton bone
> How she gnawed it
> How she clawed it
> When she felt herself alone.

Girls are cruellest to themselves.
Someone like Emily Brontë,
who remained a girl all her life despite her body as a woman,

had cruelty drifted up in all the cracks of her like spring snow.
We can see her ridding herself of it at various times
with a gesture like she used to brush the carpet.

Reason with him and then whip him!
was her instruction (age six) to her father
regarding brother Branwell.

And when she was 14 and bitten by a rabid dog she strode (they
    say)
into the kitchen and taking red-hot tongs from the back of the
    stove applied
them directly to her arm.

16

Cauterization of Heathcliff took longer.
More than thirty years in the time of the novel,
from the April evening when he runs out the back door of the
    kitchen
and vanishes over the moor

because he overheard half a sentence of Catherine's
('It would degrade me to marry Heathcliff')
until the wild morning

when the servant finds him stark dead and grinning
on his rainsoaked bed upstairs in Wuthering Heights.
Heathcliff is a pain devil.

If he had stayed in the kitchen
long enough to hear the other half of Catherine's sentence
('so he will never know how I love him')

Heathcliff would have been set free.
But Emily knew how to catch a devil.
She put into him in place of a soul

the constant cold departure of Catherine from his nervous
    system
every time he drew a breath or moved thought.
She broke all his moments in half,

with the kitchen door standing open.
I am not unfamiliar with this half-life.
But there is more to it than that.

Heathcliff's sexual despair
arose out of no such experience in the life of Emily Brontë,
so far as we know. Her question,

which concerns the years of inner cruelty that can twist a person
    into a pain devil,
came to her in a kindly firelit kitchen
('kichin' in Emily's spelling) where she

and Charlotte and Anne peeled potatoes together
and made up stories with the old house dog Keeper at their feet.
There is a fragment

of a poem she wrote in 1839
(about six years before *Wuthering Heights*) that says:

> That iron man was born like me
> And he was once an ardent boy:
> He must have felt in infancy
> The glory of a summer sky.

Who is the iron man?
My mother's voice cuts across me,
from the next room where she is lying on the sofa.

Is that you dear?
Yes Ma.
Why don't you turn on a light in there?

Out the kitchen window I watch the steely April sun
jab its last cold yellow streaks
across a dirty silver sky.
Okay Ma. What's for supper?

LIBERTY

Liberty means different things to different people.
I have never liked lying in bed in the morning.
Law did.
My mother does.

But as soon as the morning light hits my eyes I want to be out in
    it –
moving along the moor
into the first blue currents and cold navigation of everything
    awake.

I hear my mother in the next room turn and sigh and sink
    deeper.
I peel the stale cage of sheets off my legs
and I am free.

Out on the moor all is brilliant and hard after a night of frost.
The light plunges straight up from the ice to a blue hole at the
    top of the sky.
Frozen mud crunches underfoot. The sound

startles me back into the dream I was having
this morning when I awoke,
one of those nightlong sweet dreams of lying in Law's

arms like a needle in water – it is a physical effort
to pull myself out of his white silk hands
as they slide down my dream hips – I

turn and face into the wind
and begin to run.
Goblins, devils and death stream behind me.

In the days and months after Law left
I felt as if the sky was torn off my life.
I had no home in goodness any more.

To see the love between Law and me
turn into two animals gnawing and craving through one
    another
towards some other hunger was terrible.

Perhaps this is what people mean by original sin, I thought.
But what love could be prior to it?
What is prior?

What is love?
My questions were not original.
Nor did I answer them.

Mornings when I meditated
I was presented with a nude glimpse of my lone soul,
not the complex mysteries of love and hate.

But the Nudes are still as clear in my mind
as pieces of laundry that froze on the clothesline overnight.
There were in all thirteen of them.

Nude #2. Woman caught in a cage of thorns.
Big glistening brown thorns with black stains on them
where she twists this way and that way

unable to stand upright.
Nude #3. Woman with a single great thorn implanted in her
    forehead.
She grips it in both hands

endeavouring to wrench it out.
Nude #4. Woman on a blasted landscape
backlit in red like Hieronymus Bosch.

Covering her head and upper body is a hellish contraption
like the top half of a crab.
With arms crossed as if pulling off a sweater

she works hard at dislodging the crab.
It was about this time
I began telling Dr Haw

about the Nudes. She said,
When you see these horrible images why do you stay with them?
Why keep watching? Why not

go away? I was amazed.
Go away where? I said.
This still seems to me a good question.

But by now the day is wide open and a strange young April light
is filling the moor with gold milk.
I have reached the middle

where the ground goes down into a depression and fills with
    swampy water.
It is frozen.
A solid black pane of moor life caught in its own night attitudes.

Certain wild gold arrangements of weed are visible deep in the
    black.
Four naked alder trunks rise straight up from it
and sway in the blue air. Each trunk

where it enters the ice radiates a map of silver pressures —
thousands of hair-thin cracks catching the white of the light
like a jailed face

catching grins through the bars.
Emily Brontë has a poem about a woman in jail who says

                A messenger of Hope, comes every night to me
                And offers, for short life, eternal Liberty.

I wonder what kind of Liberty this is.
Her critics and commentators say she means death
or a visionary experience that prefigures death.

They understand her prison
as the limitations placed on a clergyman's daughter
by nineteenth-century life in a remote parish on a cold moor

in the north of England.
They grow impatient with the extreme terms in which she
    figures prison life.
'In so much of Brontë's work

the self-dramatizing and posturing of these poems teeters
on the brink of a potentially bathetic melodrama,'
says one. Another

refers to 'the cardboard sublime' or her caught world.
I stopped telling my psychotherapist about the Nudes
when I realized I had no way to answer her question,

Why keep watching?
Some people watch, that's all I can say.
There is nowhere else to go,

no ledge to climb up to.
Perhaps I can explain this to her if I wait for the right moment,
as with a very difficult sister.

'On that mind time and experience alone could work:
to the influence of other intellects it was not amenable,'
wrote Charlotte of Emily.

I wonder what kind of conversation these two had
over breakfast at the parsonage.
'My sister Emily

was not a person of demonstrative character,' Charlotte
    emphasizes,
'nor one on the recesses of whose mind and feelings,
even those nearest and dearest to her could,

with impunity, intrude unlicensed ...' Recesses were many.
One autumn day in 1845 Charlotte
'accidentally lighted on a MS volume of verse in my sister
    Emily's handwriting'.

It was a small (4 × 6) notebook
with a dark red cover marked 6d.
and contained 44 poems in Emily's minute hand.

Charlotte had known Emily wrote verse
but felt 'more than surprise' at its quality.
'Not at all like the poetry women generally write.'

Further surprise awaited Charlotte when she read Emily's
    novel,
not least for its foul language.
She gently probes this recess

in her Editor's Preface to *Wuthering Heights*.
'A large class of readers, likewise, will suffer greatly
from the introduction into the pages of this work

of words printed with all their letters,
which it has become the custom to represent by the initial and
    final letter only – a blank
line filling the interval.'

Well, there are different definitions of Liberty.
Love is freedom, Law was fond of saying.
I took this to be more a wish than a thought

and changed the subject.
But blank lines do not say nothing.
As Charlotte puts it,

'The practice of hinting by single letters those expletives
with which profane and violent persons are wont to garnish
    their discourse,
strikes me as a proceeding which,

however well meant, is weak and futile.
I cannot tell what good it does – what feeling it spares –
what horror it conceals.'

I turn my steps and begin walking back over the moor
towards home and breakfast.
It is a two-way traffic,

the language of the unsaid. My favourite pages
of *The Collected Works of Emily Brontë*
are the notes at the back

recording small adjustments made by Charlotte
to the text of Emily's verse,
which Charlotte edited for publication after Emily's death.
'*Prison* for *strongest* [in Emily's hand] altered to *lordly* by
    Charlotte.'

HERO

I can tell by the way my mother chews her toast
whether she had a good night
and is about to say a happy thing
or not.

Not.
She puts her toast down on the side of her plate.
You know you can pull the drapes in that room, she begins.

This is a coded reference to one of our oldest arguments,
from what I call The Rules Of Life series.
My mother always closes her bedroom drapes tight before
    going to bed at night.

I open mine as wide as possible.
I like to see everything, I say.
What's there to see?

Moon. Air. Sunrise.
All that light on your face in the morning. Wakes you up.
I like to wake up.

At this point the drapes argument has reached a delta
and may advance along one of three channels.
There is the What You Need Is a Good Night's Sleep channel,

the Stubborn As Your Father channel
and random channel.
More toast? I interpose strongly, pushing back my chair.

Those women! says my mother with an exasperated rasp.
Mother has chosen random channel.
Women?

Complaining about rape all the time –
I see she is tapping one furious finger on yesterday's newspaper
lying beside the grape jam.

The front page has a small feature
about a rally for International Women's Day –
have you had a look at the Sears Summer Catalogue?

Nope.
Why, it's a disgrace! Those bathing suits –
cut way up to here! (she points) No wonder!

You're saying women deserve to get raped
because Sears bathing suit ads
have high-cut legs? Ma, are you serious?

Well someone has to be responsible.
Why should women be responsible for male desire? My voice is
    high.
Oh I see you're one of Them.

One of Whom? My voice is very high. Mother vaults it.
And whatever did you do with that little tank suit you had last
    year the green one?
It looked so smart on you.

The frail fact drops on me from a great height
that my mother is afraid.
She will be eighty years old this summer.

Her tiny sharp shoulders hunched in the blue bathrobe
make me think of Emily Brontë's little merlin hawk Hero
that she fed bits of bacon at the kitchen table when Charlotte
    wasn't around.

So Ma, we'll go – I pop up the toaster
and toss a hot slice of pumpernickel lightly across onto her
    plate –
visit Dad today? She eyes the kitchen clock with hostility.

Leave at eleven, home again by four? I continue.
She is buttering her toast with jagged strokes.
Silence is assent in our code. I go into the next room to phone
    the taxi.

My father lives in a hospital for patients who need chronic care
about 50 miles from here.
He suffers from a kind of dementia

characterized by two sorts of pathological change
first recorded in 1907 by Alois Alzheimer.
First, the presence in cerebral tissue

of a spherical formation known as neuritic plaque,
consisting mainly of degenerating brain cells.
Second, neurofibrillary snarlings

in the cerebral cortex and in the hippocampus.
There is no known cause or cure.
Mother visits him by taxi once a week

for the last five years.
Marriage is for better or for worse, she says,
this is the worse.

So about an hour later we are in the taxi
shooting along empty country roads towards town.
The April light is clear as an alarm.

As we pass them it gives a sudden sense of every object
existing in space on its own shadow.
I wish I could carry this clarity with me

into the hospital where distinctions tend to flatten and coalesce.
I wish I had been nicer to him before he got crazy.
These are my two wishes.

It is hard to find the beginning of dementia.
I remember a night about ten years ago
when I was talking to him on the telephone.

It was a Sunday night in winter.
I heard his sentences filling up with fear.
He would start a sentence – about weather, lose his way, start
    another.
It made me furious to hear him floundering –

my tall proud father, former World War II navigator!
It made me merciless.
I stood on the edge of the conversation,

watching him thrash about for cues,
offering none,
and it came to me like a slow avalanche

that he had no idea who he was talking to.
Much colder today I guess ...
his voice pressed into the silence and broke off,

snow falling on it.
There was a long pause while snow covered us both.
Well I won't keep you,

he said with sudden desperate cheer as if sighting land.
I'll say goodnight now,
I won't run up your bill. Goodbye.

Goodbye.
Goodbye. Who are you?
I said into the dial tone.

At the hospital we pass down long pink halls
through a door with a big window
and a combination lock (5–25–3)

to the west wing, for chronic care patients.
Each wing has a name.
The chronic wing is Our Golden Mile

although mother prefers to call it The Last Lap.
Father sits strapped in a chair which is tied to the wall
in a room of other tied people tilting at various angles.

My father tilts least, I am proud of him.
Hi Dad how y'doing?
His face cracks open it could be a grin or rage

and looking past me he issues a stream of vehemence at the air.
My mother lays her hand on his.
Hello love, she says. He jerks his hand away. We sit.

Sunlight flocks through the room.
Mother begins to unpack from her handbag the things she has
    brought for him,
grapes, arrowroot biscuits, humbugs.

He is addressing strenuous remarks to someone in the air
    between us.
He uses a language known only to himself,
made of snarls and syllables and sudden wild appeals.

Once in a while some old formula floats up through the wash –
You don't say! or Happy birthday to you! –
but no real sentence

for more than three years now.
I notice his front teeth are getting black.
I wonder how you clean the teeth of mad people.

He always took good care of his teeth. My mother looks up.
She and I often think two halves of one thought.
Do you remember that gold-plated toothpick

you sent him from Harrod's the summer you were in London?
    she asks.
Yes I wonder what happened to it.
Must be in the bathroom somewhere.

She is giving him grapes one by one.
They keep rolling out of his huge stiff fingers.
He used to be a big man, over six feet tall and strong,

but since he came to hospital his body has shrunk to the merest
    bone house –
except the hands. The hands keep growing.
Each one now as big as a boot in Van Gogh,

they go lumbering after the grapes in his lap.
But now he turns to me with a rush of urgent syllables
that break off on a high note – he waits,

staring into my face. That quizzical look.
One eyebrow at an angle.
I have a photograph taped to my fridge at home.

It shows his World War II air crew posing in front of the plane.
Hands firmly behind backs, legs wide apart,
chins forward.

Dressed in the puffed flying suits
with a wide leather strap pulled tight through the crotch.
They squint into the brilliant winter sun of 1942.

It is dawn.
They are leaving Dover for France.
My father on the far left is the tallest airman,

with his collar up,
one eyebrow at an angle.
The shadowless light makes him look immortal,

for all the world like someone who will not weep again.
He is still staring into my face.
Flaps down! I cry.
His black grin flares once and goes out like a match.

HOT

Hot blue moonlight down the steep sky.
I wake too fast from a cellar of hanged puppies
with my eyes pouring into the dark.
Fumbling

and slowly
consciousness replaces the bars.
Dreamtails and angry liquids

swim back down to the middle of me.
It is generally anger dreams that occupy my nights now.
This is not uncommon after loss of love –

blue and black and red blasting the crater open.
I am interested in anger.
I clamber along to find the source.

My dream was of an old woman lying awake in bed.
She controls the house by a system of light bulbs strung above
    her on wires.
Each wire has a little black switch.

One by one the switches refuse to turn the bulbs on.
She keeps switching and switching
in rising tides of very hot anger.

Then she creeps out of bed to peer through lattices
at the rooms of the rest of the house.
The rooms are silent and brilliantly lit

and full of huge furniture beneath which crouch
small creatures – not quite cats not quite rats
licking their narrow red jaws

under a load of time.
I want to be beautiful again, she whispers
but the great overlit rooms tick emptily

as a deserted ocean liner and now behind her in the dark
a rustling sound, comes –
My pyjamas are soaked.

Anger travels through me, pushes aside everything else in my
      heart,
pouring up the vents.
Every night I wake to this anger,

the soaked bed,
the hot pain box slamming me each way I move.
I want justice. Slam.

I want an explanation. Slam.
I want to curse the false friend who said I love you forever.
      Slam.
I reach up and switch on the bedside lamp. Night springs

out the window and is gone over the moor.
I lie listening to the light vibrate in my ears
and thinking about curses.

Emily Brontë was good at cursing
Falsity and bad love and the deadly pain of alteration are
    constant topics in her verse.

> Well, thou hast paid me back my love!
> But if there be a God above
> Whose arm is strong, whose word is true,
> This hell shall wring thy spirit too!

The curses are elaborate:

> There go, Deceiver, go! My hand is streaming wet;
> My heart's blood flows to buy the blessing – To forget!
> Oh could that lost heart give back, back again to thine,
> One tenth part of the pain that clouds my dark decline!

But they do not bring her peace:

> Vain words, vain frenzied thoughts! No ear can hear me call –
> Lost in the vacant air my frantic curses fall ...

> Unconquered in my soul the Tyrant rules me still –
> *Life* bows to my control, but *Love* I cannot kill!

Her anger is a puzzle.
It raises many questions in me,
to see love treated with such cold and knowing contempt

by someone who rarely left home
'except to go to church or take a walk on the hills'
(Charlotte tells us) and who

had no more intercourse with Haworth folk
that 'a nun has
of the country people who sometimes pass her convent gates.'

How did Emily come to lose faith in humans?
She admired their dialects, studied their genealogies,
'but with them she rarely exchanged a word'.

Her introvert nature shrank from shaking hands with someone
    she met on the moor.
What did Emily know of lovers' lies or cursive human faith?
Among her biographers

is one who conjectures she bore or aborted a child
during her six-month stay in Halifax,
but there is no evidence at all for such an event

and the more general consensus is that Emily did not touch a
    man in her 31 years.
Banal sexism aside,
I find myself tempted

to read *Wuthering Heights* as one thick stacked act of revenge
for all that life withheld from Emily.
But the poetry shows traces of a deeper explanation.

As if anger could be a kind of vocation for some women.
It is a chilly thought.

> The heart is dead since infancy.
> Unwept for let the body go.

Suddenly cold I reach down and pull the blanket back up to my
    chin.
The vocation of anger is not mine.
I know my source.

It is stunning, it is a moment like no other,
when one's lover comes in and says I do not love you anymore.
I switch off the lamp and lie on my back,

thinking about Emily's cold young soul.
Where does unbelief begin?
When I was young

there were degrees of certainty.
I could say, Yes I know that I have two hands.
Then one day I awakened on a planet of people whose hands
    occasionally disappear –

From the next room I hear my mother shift and sigh and settle
back down under the doorsill of sleep.
Out the window the moon is just a cold bit of silver gristle low
    on fading banks of sky.

> Our guests are darkly lodged, I whispered, gazing through
> The vault ...

THOU

The question I am left with is the question of her loneliness.
And I prefer to put it off.
It is morning.

Astonished light is washing over the moor from north to east.
I am walking into the light.
One way to put off loneliness is to interpose God.

Emily had a relationship on this level with someone she calls
    Thou.
She describes Thou as awake like herself all night
and full of strange power.

Thou woos Emily with a voice that comes out of the night
   wind.
Thou and Emily influence one another in the darkness,
playing near and far at once.

She talks about a sweetness that 'proved us one'.
I am uneasy with the compensatory model of female religious
   experience and yet,
there is no question,

it would be sweet to have a friend to tell things to at night,
without the terrible sex price to pay.
This is a childish idea, I know.

My education, I have to admit, has been gappy.
The basic rules of male–female relations
were imparted atmospherically in our family,

no direct speech allowed.
I remember one Sunday I was sitting in the backseat of the car.
Father in front.

We were waiting in the driveway for mother,
who came around the corner of the house
and got into the passenger side of the car

dressed in a yellow Chanel suit and black high heels.
Father glanced sideways at her.
Showing a good bit of leg today Mother, he said

in a voice which I (age eleven) thought odd.
I stared at the back of her head waiting for what she would say.
Her answer would clear this up.

But she just laughed a strange laugh with ropes all over it.
Later that summer I put this laugh together with another laugh
I overheard as I was going upstairs.

She was talking on the telephone in the kitchen.
Well a woman would be just as happy with a kiss on the cheek
most of the time but YOU KNOW MEN,

she was saying. Laugh.
Not ropes, thorns.
I have arrived at the middle of the moor

where the ground goes down into a low swampy place.
The swamp water is frozen solid.
Bits of gold weed

have etched themselves
on the underside of the ice like messages.

> I'll come when thou art saddest,
> Laid alone in the darkened room;
> When the mad day's mirth has vanished,
> And the smile of joy is banished,
>
> I'll come when the heart's real feeling
> Has entire, unbiased sway,
> And my influence o'er thee stealing
> Grief deepening, joy congealing,
> Shall bear thy soul away.
>
> Listen! 'tis just the hour,
> The awful time for thee:
> Does thou not feel upon thy soul
> A flood of strange sensations roll,
> Forerunners of a sterner power,
> Heralds of me?

Very hard to read, the messages that pass
between Thou and Emily.
In this poem she reverses their roles,

speaking not *as* the victim but *to* the victim.
It is chilling to watch Thou move upon thou,
who lies alone in the dark waiting to be mastered.

It is a shock to realize that this low, slow collusion
of master and victim within one voice
is a rationale

for the most awful loneliness of the poet's hour.
She has reversed the roles of thou and Thou
not as a display of power

but to force out of herself some pity
for this soul trapped in glass,
which is her true creation.

Those nights lying alone
are not discontinuous with this cold hectic dawn.
It is who I am.

Is it a vocation of anger?
Why construe silence
as the Real Presence?

Why stoop to kiss this doorstep?
Why be unstrung and pounded flat and pine away
imagining someone vast to whom I may vent the swell of my
    soul?

Emily was fond of Psalm 130.
'My soul waiteth on Thou more than they that watch for the
    morning,
I say more than they that watch for the morning.'

I like to believe that for her the act of watching provided a
    shelter,
that her collusion with Thou gave ease to anger and desire:
'In Thou they are quenched as a fire of thorns,' says the
    psalmist.

But for myself I do not believe this, I am not quenched —
with Thou or without Thou I find no shelter.
I am my own Nude.

And Nudes have a difficult sexual destiny.
I have watched this destiny disclose itself
in its jerky passage from girl to woman to who I am now,

from love to anger to this cold marrow,
from fire to shelter to fire.
What is the opposite of believing in Thou —

merely not believing in Thou? No. That is too simple.
That is to prepare a misunderstanding.
I want to speak more clearly.

Perhaps the Nudes are the best way.
Nude #5. Deck of cards.
Each card is made of flesh.

The living cards are days of a woman's life.
I see a great silver needle go flashing right through the deck once
    from end to end.
Nude #6 I cannot remember.

Nude #7. White room whose walls,
having neither planes nor curves nor angles,
are composed of a continuous satiny white membrane

like the flesh of some interior organ of the moon.
It is a living surface, almost wet.
Lucency breathes in and out.

Rainbows shudder across it.
And around the walls of the room a voice goes whispering,
Be very careful. Be very careful.

Nude #8. Black disc on which the fires of all the winds
are attached in a row.
A woman stands on the disc

amid the winds whose long yellow silk flames
flow and vibrate up through her.
Nude #9. Transparent loam.

Under the loam a woman has dug a long deep trench.
Into the trench she is placing small white forms, I don't know
    what they are.
Nude #10. Green thorn of the world poking up

alive through the heart of a woman
who lies on her back on the ground.
The thorn is exploding

its green blood above her in the air.
Everything it is it has, the voice says.
Nude #11. Ledge in outer space.

Space is bluish black and glossy as solid water
and moving very fast in all directions,
shrieking past the woman who stands pinned

to nothing by its pressure.
She peers and glances for some way to go, trying to lift her hand
    but cannot.
Nude #12. Old pole in the wind.

Cold currents are streaming over it
and pulling out
into ragged long horizontal black lines

some shreds of ribbon
attached to the pole.
I cannot see how they are attached –

notches? staples? nails? All of a sudden the wind changes
and all the black shreds rise straight up in the air
and tie themselves into knots,

then untie and float down.
The wind is gone.
It waits.

By this time, midway through winter,
I had become entirely fascinated with my spiritual melodrama.
Then it stopped.

Days passed, months passed and I saw nothing.
I continued to peer and glance, sitting on the rug in front of my
    sofa
in the curtainless morning

with my nerves open to the air like something skinned.
I saw nothing.
Outside the window spring storms came and went.

April snow folded its huge white paws over doors and porches.
I watched a chunk of it lean over the roof and break off
and fall and I thought,

How slow! as it glided soundlessly past,
but still – nothing. No nudes.
No Thou.

A great icicle formed on the railing of my balcony
so I drew up close to the window and tried peering through the
    icicle,
hoping to trick myself into some interior vision,

but all I saw
was the man and woman in the room across the street
making their bed and laughing.

I stopped watching.
I forgot about Nudes.
I lived my life,

which felt like a switched-off TV.
Something had gone through me and out and I could not own
    it.
'No need now to tremble for the hard frost and the keen wind.

Emily does not feel them,'
wrote Charlotte the day after burying her sister.
Emily had shaken free.

A soul can do that.
Whether it goes to join Thou and sit on the porch for all
    eternity
enjoying jokes and kisses and beautiful cold spring evenings,

you and I will never know. But I can tell you what I saw.
Nude #13 arrived when I was not watching for it.
It came at night.

Very much like Nude #1.
And yet utterly different.
I saw a high hill and on it a form shaped against hard air.

It could have been just a pole with some old cloth attached,
but as I came closer
I saw it was a human body

trying to stand against winds so terrible that the flesh was
    blowing off the bones.
And there was no pain.
The wind

was cleansing the bones.
They stood forth silver and necessary.
It was not my body, nor a woman's body, it was the body of us
    all.
It walked out of the light.

KAY ADSHEAD *The Slug Sabbatical*

with love to Peter Carr

Waiting at Hammersmith bus station
Returning from a Sabbatical from life
I invited a small, frail
Skin-shedding, human male
To kiss me.

Believing me legless, he declined.
Anyway, he had no lips to speak of.
But I found my tongue (after a search)
Cracked and furred
And licking the scaly hole
Beneath his nose
Inflamed him.

The Sabbatical was over!
Tongues being thicker, fatter, softer
And wetter
Than I remember.

                    *

We met outside Mansion House tube station
It was a hot afternoon.
He was late, but clean
Shedding skin like soapflakes
All the way to the pub.

We sipped warm beer
Swapping bony kisses

His long, pale, monk fingers
Scratching my shoulder

And, while I, being an open sort,
Told him
Everything,

He sat shedding skin silently
Till closing time

Leaving a trail like ash
To the optics and back.

*

Outside the day was a lizard
Tumbleweed blew between my legs.

We kissed once more
His tongue marinated now in stale beer

Intimacy coming in different flavours.

*

Alone again and underground
In love and out of breath
His kisses limpet-like still at my throat –

I arrived just in time
To watch the train door slide shut slyly.
And in an Act of Madness
(Love makes you mad!)
Thrust out my bag (fish skin)
Trapping it, as the train smirked off,
And on the other side of its greasy glass
(I was running now)

Just caught the eye (seal-like)
Of a tradesperson in corporation green

And waders

Helpfully tugging
Showering raindrops
In thin silver darts
From his shiny black braids

Leaving a rainbow on the carriage window.

*

Night! And a knock!
I lick my lips.
The Skin-Shedding Man.

'Come in.'
On the mat a pyramid of skin.
He blinks
And worse, his nostrils twitch.
His eyes make for the ceiling
And its seven water marks.

'I didn't realize you live ...'
'Underground?'

In the vestibule
The earth squelches underfoot
I take him to the river
(Where else?)

*

Higher up, where the black air boils
– Only a stone's throw –
Electrical lights scream and shimmy

And all is normalcy
And Saturday-Night Julio Iglesias
At 'The Drowned Bat'
Where I watch the regulation human males
– Two arms, legs, heads
One plastic pint pot for the pissing in –
With a warm, wet, aching heart
Harking back to before ...
Before the Sabbatical

And Before the Before.

Suddenly the shale splutters.
Dust rises, chortles and then coughs
It's the Skin-Shedder!
Genie-like against the stars –
The Skin-Shedder!
Shinning the steep slope
Carefully bearing doubles!

And I'm caught out!
Submerged
A good 12 feet from the river's edge
Oozing and luminous

'A hippopotamus ...'
He jokes, swallowing doubts
As I haul myself breathless to the bank.

He's strangely animated
His eyes dilate
He won't allow silences

Except when his
Whisky and American Dry tonight-tongue
Excavates.

And I am silky submitting
Dampness from the neck down
Allowing his one free hand to fore-play –

River silt being the perfect lubricant.

*

Crri-i-ck! The key turns scratchy in the lock.
The mossy door whines ... 'home'
And the stench!
Pinning us gagging to the night –
Sudden putrefaction and pot pourri.

Remember it had been a long Sabbatical
The Adjudicating Council strict but fair
Visitors were forbidden.

'Come in'

Studiously I avoid his gaze
Reach in the kitchen cupboard for the Haze
Ps-s-s-st. That's better!
Mmmmn. Air-fresher! –
'Sudden-Springtime'.
(A mist over the unease.)

'Crocus Coffee? Tulip Tea?'

He turns his lipless smile on me.

Round the lip of the cafetière
A fat, green slug perambulates
Catching the Skin-Shedder's eye.
His smile shreds.
He shudders –
A sudden avalanche of skin.

Leaving a white ravine on the kitchen floor.

Quick as a flash
I tear a scrap
Of Izal bog-roll
The last existing flat pack in the world
A keepsake of a finer time

And hi-jack the little chap

Leaning over the lavatory bowl
Watching him spiral helpless in the spumy foam
I note:
He invests all but his last second as a slug
In a powerful eyeless reproach.

*

The Living-In Room
Two steaming mugs.
The Skin-Shedder –
Sitting on a sofa
As if it was the most natural thing
In the world –
Sips without lips.
He sucks
A smoking infusion
And I kneel
Head in the clouds
Pores opening
And inhale!
The ash bark and dipper's nest, sleet tea
While his fingers unbutton my frock.

As I've already said
His nails are long

From cuticle to tip
A good 8 inches
And serrated
Unbuttoning is a fiddly operation.

Yoist! – goes the brassière –
Up and over
Curious breasts
Sprung
To the moaning air.

My nipples chirrup
He swoops
I note:
Ears are the same opaque purply white
Found in the stalk of a young red cabbage
And
Yes!
Tongues are in fact
Wet!
And strong! –
And long! –

And a kissed breast
Is Pure Poetry
As is sucking, licking, nibbling, biting,

But oh it's late
And dangerous!
Already the sofa is starting to bubble
And what's that seeping under the door?

'Shall we ...'

Whose voice is that
Brewed and cavernous?

No. Further –
From the bottom of a fetid well
Or further still –
Through the crust, the mantle
To the steaming inner core
From the broiled and bilious centre of the self.

And so we repair to the bedroom
Where it will be more comfortable.

As I turn off the light
I note:
All that is left of me in the Living-In Room
Is a damp patch on the shag pile.
Unlike the Skin-Shedder
Who tell-tales all his way to my pillow.

          *

Two steps down
Further underground
Pitch blackness
The smell of tinned soup
The floor hot and gummy
So that his soles stick.

Zzssrip! A struck match.
The astonished air spits back.

It's a grotto is it?
Or is it a shrine?
In the atmosphere something ferments
Old whisperings have left their sediments
(Prayers? Offered up to Neptune's moons
Only to splat against the ceiling and ooze back)

And what's that sticky substance on the walls?

In the corners
A phallus fungus
(The noble stink-horn)
Propagates itself
Against the skirting board.

And there are hundreds
Hundreds and hundreds
Far more than I remember
Hooded, spongy and purple

Waving now in the warm draught from the door.

There's an altar slightly to our left
(Or is it a dressing-up table?)
And a candle, tall and formal
Which I light.

Is it a river cave?
A-spangle with fresh-water shells –
Is it?

He stands transfixed
Lipless and illuminated
Like a stern, stone saint

But remember the soft ground?
The Skin-Shedder
Is starting to sink.

At some point
A strip of 2 by 4
Was laid out across the boggy floor
From door to bed
For Easy Passage

Shoes – winklepickers, flip-flops and brogues –
Remain
Cemented by candlelight
Abandoned
Souvenirs of many a two-legged
Communicant,

But that was all Before
And other times
The shoes are fossilized.

There had been no recent bipeds
Chancing their arm
No, not for centuries
(Another stipulation)
And centuries an under-estimation

And I rarely slept in the room
I rarely slept
Spending up most of the Sabbatical
Dragging my stump
Up and down
The draughty vestibule

The Skin-Shedder goldfishes
At last ...
I hear him say
'Nice pad'
Determining
He walks the plank.

I slither behind religiously
Kissing his calves.

(It's Saturday so I'm legless
The calls upon the National Health are desperate
False limbs go back at the weekend.)

*

We lie –
On my
Posture-sprung
Sarcophagus
Crusted with lichen and liverwort
An eiderdown of mollusc and marsh violet
By the wild blue Iris –

A lady and her knight

Waiting somehow

As if someone had pressed her pause button
(Or for the Dark Ages to pass).

The bed – in other words –
What can I say?
I let the rat-tailed maggots have their day
(See the corpses)
(See the spatter of undigested candlewick).

The walls are shiny and slippering
Oil-slick orange and indigo
They glow.

Here and there
A horny pea-cockle winks.

The spores on the ceiling make pictures –
Here's an illustrated map of Japan

See the bridge, the lake
The overhanging willow tree

Why does the little geisha girl
Smirk behind her parasol?

To this brown stain
That I suppose time made
I took my magic marker and gave horns
A tail, fire breath
Even a bubble shouting 'Sea serpents rule'.

I joined up the rams horn shells
And found:

A man
On a bike
Smoking a pipe

What a surprise.

The Skin-Shedder coughs
He's getting cramp
Land-lubbers find it hard
To deal with damp.

Up I bounce
And over
Po-go sticking
In the squall –

Stopping to catch my breath at the mirror.

Howzat?

Look at me panting!
I'm luminescent on the other side of the glass.

Hyperventilation should be bottled
Seeing as it brings the colour back.

And there are other bottles here
In the bedroom

Apart from the dusty Milk of Magnesia
And the sticky-topped Veno's Cough Mixture

Tiny diamond-cut amber phials
Flasks, green and globular
With ruby tear-drop stoppers

Pitchers, purple and impossible
Being thinner than air
Gold-speckled
But lead-bottomed.

Bus trips on the No. 74
Dropped me at the Apothecary's door

The dressing-up table groans and buckles
(Hear it ...)
So many, but each label says the same:
Though here and there
A single word may change
Directions: To promote leg growth
Apply sparingly to stumps.

Something breathes
In the black-spotted glass
The Skin-Shedder's ribs
Appear to heave –

Something sighs ...
How patient his reflection lies

And what a perfect composition –
Pink candlelight, flickering foreground

Playing

On one long, loose, lilac arm;

Figure, recumbent, in burgundies and brown
Lost, almost, against the wash background –

Oh!

And I had thought
The Skin-Shedder
No oil painting

Though it's a shame
His head's cut off

Another cough
From the bed
Another dry cough

Forget the sticky Veno's Mixture
I am all Elixir
All embrocation

I will rub myself
Well in
And over
The reflection of the Skin-Shedding Man

Dripping stump
Over bones

For his stillness
(His absolute stillness)
Moves me

And my desire
Is slimy.

We undress.

Out of a top, tight, squeaky drawer
I take the polyurethane –
With safety-stitched zinc gusset
High-waisted with nipple braces
Elasticated and electronically
Impregnated with *Spermazonk* –

Peace of Mind Panterlings

They are the latest thing

Like Grandma's plastic rain bonnet
In a little perspex wallet
With a popper

They parachute
To suit
And stretch to fit
All sizes

The Skin-Shedder's already wearing his
(How small his penis is).

*

LIGHT!

From the surface
Security light
Turning itself on

A shaft

Through the barred air-grille.

'Keep still'

The Skin-Shedder breaking his silence
Sweats

Footsteps!
So there is something to worry about
The security system is too highly sensitized
(You have to watch what you say)
A large moth (albeit a pretty one)
Entering its zone can turn it on.

And look at the Skin-Shedder
Trembling.
He's like a nervous bride
His skin confetties
Has he butterflies inside?

'Nn-nnnnnnnnn!'
He jumps
I can (actually) see
His adrenaline pump

His sweat crystal
His fear (icy).
Even the footsteps freeze.

'Nnnnnn!'
From the sky
The last Pterodactyl's
Hopeless mating cry?

For she lives still
On the aluminium mountain
Picking flesh juicy off the bones
Of documentary film crews

'Nnnnnn!'
A siren
But not of this vicinity
It hit a top B flat
Ours is a bottom C

The Skin-Shedder sighs
What a relief!

An urgent call
The other side of town

And what the footsteps call
'A shout'.

They shuffle
A shiny toe-cap
Kicks the frosty rubble

And we were a hot tip
The Legless Woman and the Skin-Shedding Man
The feet up top
Are seriously pissed-off

A second's digging-in of heels
A stomp
On the sole
A government issue stamp
(Silhouette of a lamb)

And then
They scarper.

Silence.

The Skin-Shedder farts
A little flurry of flakes
In the draught
From his fat rear end

And
Suddenly –
Blubs

His flesh
A quivery mess
Waxy and white
(And oozy)
His red eyes leak
Snot pours from his nose

A little yellow putrid essence
Fizzes under his toenails
Leaving an icing of scum
Over his upturned feet
Curious this
(The air's sour!
Leakage from another orifice?)

And from his ears too
A stinking yellowy goo.

From the hole in his face
Come bubbles
That pop
Then froth
Then drizzle down his chin
And what a din!

Wet sobs
And an air-shatteringly soft wail.

One of his nails
Has broken off.
(Too much angst
And clawing)

See it!
It lies in the bog
Like a razor shell.

Those talons were alluring
The ten perfectly pushed-back
Half moons
The tips
Gold-dipped.

So was his scabby dryness.

He's still
At last
But very damp.

Breathing –
Just
Grateful to be alive.

(The footsteps might have brought a sticky end
Public disembowelling happens daily)

As I slither-in
And hover-over

I note:
Gratitude
Rots

(Feels clammy?)
And smells like an old pissoir.

Cliccck –
The security light
Turning itself off!

Oh!

For a Mars bar
And a hot bath

For back in the sudden candlelight
The Skin-Shedder
Looks like a corpse!

  *

We make miserable love
A necrophilia
A kind of cling-film coupling
The Peace of Mind Panterlings
Are a pain in the arse

You take
The penile
Polyurethane protuberance

Wet it

And with the sprong-prong
Tuck it
Quite high up the vaginal walls
In position
An impact lubricant releases
An authentic, reproduced

Vagina fragrance
And a vulva flavour

Proving more popular than peppermint

Though tests on rats
Showed increased risk of rabies
And mass suicide
Shortly after first contact.

I have three goes
It takes 17 ½ minutes.

*

Out come the slugs
With their wise smiles
Tantalised and tentacled
Understanding the air

Ten thousand
Slivery trails
Criss-cross the bog.

An advance party
Stop to examine the Skin-Shedder's broken nail

Discuss
Their pretty heads cocked and curious
And then –
They everest the bed
While Dvořák's pounding in my head.

I use music to distract
Me from the act of love
And the Skin-Shedder's shallow thrusting

Is percussive
So is our breath.

The slugs
Mount us
(My familiars)

Their soft underbellies
Cold and frilly
Slug to skin
A novel intimacy
Widely unpractised
Even frowned upon
In polite circles
(Or by Englishmen).

A large brown brother slug
Seems to sail up the Skin-Shedder's
Shrink-wrapped buttock

Storm-tossed
In the thrustings
But steady as she goes.

Another abseils his heel
Another toes.

Some 20 or 30
Light on their pads
Pas-de-deux
On the turn of a flute
Along his steep backbone.

A moan
From somewhere under?
Or rather

A sweet exhalation
While a sly sister
Circumnavigates my nipple
Leaving a soft shiny 'O'.

Slugs are nude
Absolutely
Their bare spongy undersides
Quite rude

A Creationist might argue
(Tongue in cheek)
They give God a bad name

Though their slitherings
Damp and silver on my stump
Catch the moonlight nicely.

My breath keeps coming
The Skin-Shedder too
Is moving to emission

And suddenly
There are millions
A gypsy camp
(Hear the violin?)
In the forest
Of the Skin-Shedder's gritted scalp.

Some (those with wanderlust)
Caravan the bridge of his pitted conk
(Pointy and pitted)
A pinky potholes a nostril
Antennae waving in the short warm blast
Another, plump and lazy,
Moon-bathes on a brow

A baby pleasures itself
Along a line of eyelash
Its trace
Pearlizing the lid.

Everywhere they go
Armpit, pectoral or toe
They leave their seminal dew

Even prettifying
The Skin-Shedder's plastic anus
Though I concede
A few may find the notion heinous

It being one of the new crimes

As for me
I'm drenched in slime

As usual!

Breath!

Breath!

On the clash of a cymbal

The Skin-Shedder
(Who doesn't know he's musical)

And is barely aware of the slugs
Is about to erupt

And we are no longer
He and She –
Humanity

But a rumbling slug mountain
A volcano

Wusssssssssssssssssssssssssssssssssssssssssssh!

A tidal river wave
Ten foot high and raging
Breaks down the bedroom door
Hinges popping like champagne corks

In its jealous roar
Instantly blasted apart
We flotsam for a second
To a full orchestra
Arms flailing

Gagging as the briny shock
Hits the back of the throat

Fortissimo.

He gurgles
His pale yellow eyes
Like marbles

(Mouthing something!)

The dressing-up table bobs by
And all the bottles
Bearing their messages
'Goodbye'

I was due for a good clear-out.

The bed
Garlanded with fronds of river weed

And swollen
Is upturned
Like Finbara's Throne

The wave
Keeps coming
White and foaming
Keeps rising

There's no point
In fighting

The slugs philosophical
Rest on the water
As peaceful as lilies

Breath!

Again!

Sucked
Ceiling air
A brown lungful
A last desperate gulpful
Before giving in
And going under

*

Down
In the underwater bedroom
I'm blind
The Skin-Shedder's wild thrashings
Have disturbed the dirt floor
To make – murk

Something cold
Slaps against my cheek

Trembling fingers find empty eye-holes
And a lolling tongue

A tennis shoe
Size 9
Once barnacled
Set sail
In the black tempest

Tenderly I braille
Its inner sole
Which comes away at my touch
Like memory

And I see birds-eye visions
A barbed-wire cage
Spinning in an infinite blue Universe
Yellow and blue

My youth is it?
On a bleached-out tennis court
When I had legs.

Love 40
He always beat me
On account of his back-hand
From which sprouted
Long dark silky hairs

Almost a fur

His toes too
Were furry
Through his shoe

He was a 3-buttocked man
A preference in those days

A little Filipino girl
Hand-stitched his tennis shorts

I ordered her
In one sharp corner
To embroider
'*M*'
For Mine.

Our rallies were colossal
He was hairier
I nimbler on my pins

For those were the days
Of toes and ankles
Two matching knotty calves
Smooth and sinewy
And a pair of amber knees

Once he let me win!

Seeking sustenance
After the match
A measly 3-setter
Shaking out the contents
Of his Karrimore
Wildly about the gravel floor
He discovered, in a fever,
His last fig roll
Was gone.

Bitter accusation followed
Although of all confectionery
I despised fig roll especially

Convinced absolutely
Of my certain guilt
Confirmed as he saw it
By my fierce sweet tooth

He brooded darkly
Through the next decade
While I, innocent,
Utterly innocent

(Honestly)

Nursed the injustice
That caused
The pins and needles
In my lower limbs

Meanwhile
His wrist and racket
(Which in time
Also grew hair
Seriously hampering his serve)
Sliced finely
Through the hot young afternoons
Till finally
They were gone.

Something rubs
Pleasantly intimate
Another scaly memory
Fished-for between my legs.

A brogue
A Size 13
Huge and hard
And slippery in my hand.

It was his
(What a whopper!
Who said
Size doesn't matter?)

The huge hard slippery man
Whose love was so immense
(At least as big as his feet)
I was impaled upon it
And up there
In the sweet stiff moaning air
Catching cloud on my tongue

I didn't need to walk
Or even talk

So never noticed
The gangrenous silence
Or my toes turning black.

The flip-flop
Panics —
What a performance!
Twisting this way
And that
Through my fingers

Desperate for the cover
Of the Quiet Years
Stuck in the bog
Where very slowly
It grew gills
(For all eventualities)
And was happy.

The Flip-Flop Man
Made me laugh
He gave up shoes
Entirely in time

Bagging them
For the Dalai Lama

Even his pair of patent courts
With the Cuban Heel

Bought for a song
At the seaside
To fox-trot
With sequinned
English ancients

Blue-rinsed
Down to their genitals
But with BO.

They'd offer sly back-handers
For a slow tango.

Barefoot in London
Very often
We'd be taken down
To the Cells
For the night

Don't ask me why.
Toes don't speak
And can't
Disturb the peace

But the street was cool
To my putrefying feet
Blue now to the shin
And the Hard City air
Had brought about

A temporary return of feeling
Below the knees
At least.

One night
Tired of turning
His pockets out
And after
A bit too much
To drink

He stumbled across
A parlour
Licensed to practise
Body puncture
In Kentish Town
By Ladbrokes.

Drawn by the scent
Of the cinnamon candles
And an incandescence
Warmed by the booze

He had his feet
Indelibly tattooed
With Jesus sandals –

Skilfully done
And with witty detail
A flaw in the thonging
They'd fool anyone –

Then headed for the hills.
Mountains even.
Looking for Reasons.

With only
An emergency
Corn-plaster kit.

I watched him
Lump in my throat
Become a dot in my life
Before needing to sit down

To take the weight
Off my feet.

          *

Sudden calm
Up top
The kicking stops
The murk melts
Mysteriously into itself

A second
And I can see.

Two painfully thin limbs
(Severed?)
Dangle dangerously limp
And still
Two fillet-of-fish feet
Ten-toed and familiar?

Half drowned
In dreams
And out of the madness
Of Blindness

I believed
That they were mine

In that moment
My own
Miraculous
And Grown Again
From the fertile river bed
My strong, young, vanished legs!

But for the buttocks!
There (attached to thighs)
And square
And unmistakably
Skin-shedding.

All about
Shoes
Or the Fossils
Of Shoes

Their skeletons
Swept from their sacred burial ground
The boggy bedroom floor
By the wild white wave

Bubble up to the surface

Here an espadrille
All the way from the Aegean –
And just out of reach

A loafer dodges my clumsy lunge

An elastic-sided Chelsea boot,
Still sharp, pricks memory
And draws blood
Pinned against a lamp-post

Somewhere sticky
By its dangerous steel toe

A Dl M floats upwards
A little slower than the rest

A Reebok
Its lace
Catching in my hair

A moccasin
The last surviving bead
Hanging from a single thread
Like a silver tear

A jolly jelly sandal!
And a Dr Scholl's

Even a brown wool
Slipper – zippered
To the ankle

Up they float
A soft glub-glub
Of bubbles
In their wake.

I can't catch them
They weave out of reach
Or slip through my fingers
Like mischievous eels

All the black lace-ups
And the Italian tan slip-ons
The suede and the suedette
The side-buckled
And the custom-stitched

The hand-finished
And the toggle-tongued

Shoes
Or the fossils of shoes
Their skeletons
Float
Up, up to the bright surface
Where they bob
In the new and shiny moonlight
With the slugs

Slug-shoe!
Slug-shoe!
Slug-shoe!

A billion bobbing
Out of the boggy subconscious

Into the oxygen
Of
Now!

A face looms
From nowhere
Strangely amphibious
There's something fishy here.

Shark's eyes
And a blue whale
Of a mouth

Or is it just the light?
Playing on the water

An optical illusion
Of the Night.

A subterranean mind
Netting a queer catch

It's the Skin-Shedder
(My stopped heart starts)
Mouthing something still
And desperate

An exclamation mark
Of bubbles rising
From the black hole in his face

Then a 'B'
An 'A' a 'C'
Of bubbles
An 'O ...'

'Bacon and Eggs
Two toasted muffins
And a pot of English
Breakfast Tea'

The Skin-Shedder
Is telling me
What he wants for breakfast

!

    *

A lipless black cave
Moist and sweet
Somewhere far back
A glimmer of wet gold –
Good teeth!

A stalactite of spit
And that tongue
Even longer now
Like a snake's

It's Sunday morning
On the wire-less
A (late) Flood Warning

I am spoon-feeding
The Skin-Shedder
Soggy CoCo Pops

(He's had a nasty shock)

His epiglottis
Defenceless as a tadpole
Quivers to the air

I wipe the warm milk
From his chin.

We're being informed
(It's the Public Information Station)
Burst river banks
In the Thames Basin
Were caused
By Mrs Jameson
Leaving a bathroom tap on
(Overnight)
In the Cairngorms

Lies!
All Lies!

Though the Skin-Shedder
Conducts a feasibility study

With a flow diagram
(And a finger) on the muddy
Kitchen table.

Outside under a pink sky
The planet's ship-wrecked.
I decide to walk him back
To Putney Bridge.

He walks
I haul and slither.

There's no buses
Not a soul's about

The silty city pavement
Warms under my belly

The park clock's stopped
But it's early

I leave the first trail of the day.

Out of the Turbulence
It seems
The small details of people's lives
Have been parcelled
With strings of river weed
And tied in trees

Or wrapped round traffic lights

Or swept in tidy piles
Uncanny this
Cuff-links in one corner
Wedding rings another
Neck-braces

False teeth
False legs.

I make a note
To loot
On the way home.

Though on Sunday Evening
The Leg man comes
In his black van.

In every street
From every house
Pairs of tights
Caught on the guttering
Wave like bunting

Welcoming us
Back Up

Back Up
To the Surface.

I inhale
It might rain later
But for now
England smells medieval
(Like a blocked drain)

At the deserted tube station
A broken blackboard
Gives the explanation
'Guard
Gone'
A white envelope
Flutters

A brass tack at the top
Addressed to – 'Us'
Or – 'Sunday Passengers'

Inside, a missive
20 pages long
And in a flowing hand

Chronicles
His last ten years
Of Guarding

And explains
Why last night
After much thought
He took it on himself
To chuck it in

(His wife sounds nice).

At the ticket machine
We tap in our requirements

The tide mark on his neck
Brings back the Night

I moisten
Suck his toes
His shoes
Lost in the fight
With the flood
(As always).

In Electro-Speak
The mechanical ticket-giver
Lisps 'I'm water-logged'

We pull a 'Proceed without Penalty' sticker
From her rusty groin

Then
Up, up to the Overground
And the light

Gripping his ankles
Arms taut and freckly
Hitching a ride
Up the cold steps
Bracing myself to the bumps –

Up to the sunny station platform
Where behind barbed wire
The coltsfoot seeds in the sidings
And the blackberry bush
Brambles
Thistles –
And the Giant Rhubarb
Waxy and thick-stemmed
Presses like great green ears
Against the mesh

The jungly click-click
Comes from the magnetic eye
Wired high in the horse-chesnut
Snapping us for the record.

The morning's Marie-Celeste
So far.
A Coke can's left
And chips in paper
Barely touched

An inky thumb-print
On a battered saveloy

Up here there's no trace of the wave.
Two sparrows
Cock and hen
Bathe in the dust

He perches on the bench
I lounge
Sun on my stumps
Head in his lap

Poking a finger in his facial hole
Making circles
Enjoying being inside
And going public.

From behind a vending machine
A sly rattle.
For one pound exactly
Popped in the slot
You can purchase
Emergency Reading Specs
Disposable (3 strengths 2 styles)
With an accompanying Russian novel
Of an impressive size
(See multi-choice)
Pre-dating 1955.
A thin young woman
Bangs the side

Hoping for a freebie
Short-sighted
And desperate for a read.

Her hair
Wispy and fair's
Grown back
Just

But all round the crown
Skirting her ears and brow

Stitches
Hem a thoughtful frown
And skull-cap her head

A Do-It-Yourself
Lobotomy
Common to the cut-backs

Outside any tube
You'll see
2 or 3
Studying neurology

For beginners
Step by step

And others
Post-operative
Still grisly
The voices gone
For good

She chats
Happily
To no one

(The operation
Wasn't a success)

Squatting in the gravel
Violin between her legs.

The train!
Faint
But unstoppable

Last night's love
Trapped
At the back of my throat
Comes suddenly back up
In an air bubble

'Hic! –

'Excuse me'

Hand over my mouth
I take the fine flesh
From the back of my hand
Between my teeth
And squeeze

But
Something deeper
(And Dostoevskian)
Bites at my bowel

I love him
Will he send me a postcard?

We rise!
I bounce from the bench
Hanging from his trouser belt
Being brave
Kissing the downy vee
At the small of his back.

The train
Hits the station
In a rage

There's no skin
At his feet!
Not a shred
Round the bench!
No powdery track
Up the steps!

And now I come to think of it
I snailed the muddy streets
All he left were footprints
Handsome and Crusoe-esque

I draw a finger
Down his spine
It squeaks.
Has he been turtle-waxed?
(He sports a sheen)
Or have the river's nutrients
Deep cleansed
And purified?

Washing
A short lifetime's
Trillion toxins
Down, down to the open sea
(And the Swedes)

You'd pay
An arm and a leg
For a whole body

Mud-rub
In Ll A.

He hops into the empty carriage
The scalped woman
Hot-foots after
Red-eyed
Glad of the company

I stick to the platform
Rooted
And mutilated

Seeing him
As he sits
Through the greater 'V'
Of her long green legs

That cough
'Goodbye'
They're off!

She has taken out
Her violin
And plays for him

He's captive.

As they turn the corner
Further up the line
And smaller

The whole train jigs
He taps his foot!
I see it
Five Judas toes
Tap! Tap!

What will have happened by Earl's Court?

Will he have danced a reel?
Hurling himself at the air
Iron-calved
And feet
Like playful salmon

Will he?

       *

He's made lace of my heart
Extremities
Finger-tips
And stump webbing
Prickle

Something sharp
(Besides the silence)
Tickles
My gut

I throw up
Onto the track

A sour bellyful
Of wave
And breakfast

Plankton on Toast
Torrential
Like a gargoyle.

Hanging over the edge
My eyes meet others

Human and staring.
My soul sweats.

A dismembered head
Still fresh
And rakish in its Guard's cap
Catches a lick of sunlight

Hardly sinewy
But for the odd fine grisly thread
Proof of the one clean slice.

We might have guessed
His annual pay rise deferred
His wife
Putting her name down as a reserve
To help on the animal liberation stall
On Sundays
Losing his snooker cue

I look for his torso
There is one
Swinging from the beeches
In pyjamas

It isn't his
He's black
The torso's blue.

*

I wriggle home
Squirm heave and wriggle
Sweating up each step

Stopping to sob
At the top

A handless woman
Washing the water line
Off her window
(Chamois leather
Clenched in camel's teeth)
Sees me and spits

Calling her 12 humpy kids
To come out and laugh
At the human worm

Back inside
And panting
I slide down the slammed door
Warm and wobbly as a jelly

Dissolving into the squelchy dark
And the familiar.

From under the sink
The place for the greens
(Formerly shoe polish)
I take a whole head
Of cabbage
Horridly heavy in my hands
Shred it
Then toss the skins
Like a mad flower girl
At a funeral

Stuffing the odd fistful
Down the back of the sofa
Dropping little piles
In each dark spidery corner

Draping tendrils
Over the Bay of Biscay print curtains
And the carved monkey lampstand
And the Bargain Buy
Oak-framed representation
Of Mary mother of God
Being led weeping
From the Place of the Skull

Then

I put the bolts on
Check the letter box

For flap

And go to bed
(For a nap)
For a week
At least.

I dream I'm at Golgotha

On the cross
Next to Jesus

What a view!
The Cosmos
Stretched purple
Each planet
Spinning
To its own dark drone

And Jesus
With Jupiter
Reflected in his eyes

(Eyes
Hot and terrible)
Turns to me
And cries

Why are you legless?
And I say ...

Flap! –

The Postman
Is it?
Bringing word
From my Skin-Shedder
In red ink

A declaration
(Scribbled)
Of Foreverness

I sleep-slither to the letterbox
Past the gorging gastropods
Mountainous and munching

Cabbage.

On the mat –
Torture!
Thrice.

My fingers tremble

A circular
Offering
Cut-price pedicures
On Thursdays

A voucher
50p off
Heeling and soling
This side of the summer solstice
(In any state-chain
Shoe Repair Shop)

And a glossy
Catalogue
Advertising
The latest
In foot spas.

Back in bed
Jesus commiserates
He's never tried a foot spa
But somebody washed his feet once.

Jeers!
A spear
(Somewhere
Unpleasant)

'Why are you legless?'

'Because ...

I am ...

The Legless ...
Woman!'

Flap!

A final demand
For Council Tax

The Crowd
Bays
(Truly)

And Jesus
Talks of Shoes
Peep-toe
Platform soles
Stiletto

And socks!
(I didn't realize
He was such
A chatterbox)

Flap!

Flap!

Flap! Flap!

Library book reminders

Entertaining on a Shoe-String
God as a Mollusc

Jesus wets his blistered lips
With a hard dry tongue.

A poison-pen letter
On lemon-scented paper
Threatening to inform
The Adjudicating Council
Of all two-legged visitors

A quote from Drain Clearance
No postcard!

No
'I love you'

Or

'That was nice
Let's do it again please
Soon'

Or even

'Hope you are
Keeping
Well
The weather here
Is ...'

I am crying
Real dream tears
The sky rolls
Red
Then
Black

My sobs thunder
The Slugs
Stop chomping

While Jesus
Yellow-eyed
And oozing

Wails ...

'I gave up
My Sabbatical
For you

You
Bastard'

*

In bed
Still
Imbibing
(Bacardi Breezers
By the bucket)

Listening to Shula Archer
Confess
To the double slaying
Of Sid and Cathy Perks.

A chocolate chip cookie –
The very last –
Mysteriously
Goes missing

Reaching down
Into the slurry –
Sheets sea-furred
(And sweaty)

I find –
The Skin;

His

Whole
As a snake's

The Skin-Shedder
As he lives
And breathes

His butter muslin
Likeness

Left
From our night
Making love

With the wave.

It's perfect
A perfect
Cobweb Cast
Each bony toe and finger
(Crêpy round the knuckle)

His penis
Gossamer now
And sweetly flaccid.

A bubble, almost,
For an Adam's apple

Rice-paper pouches
In the place of knees

His small tight lizardy head
Silky spun and gauzy.

I hold the skin
Tight and angry
In my hands

And at that moment
The sun
Breaks through
The thunderclouds

And light
Shines
Through him

Transforming light
Celestial light

He is
All light

My
Man of light

Transfigured
And
Forgiven!

I fold the skin
20 times
Small as a top pocket handkerchief
And on each crease
I plant a kiss
(20 seedling wishes)

From the dressing-up table
I take a key
Unlock the drawer
Used for cufflinks
Wedding rings
Birth/Death/Swimming
Certificates

And buttons.

And take a thin, brown
Office envelope
In the corner

Neatly print 'S.S.' –
Tuck the folded skin
Carefully inside
And licking
Seal it
(It tastes of dead horse flies)

Then put it with the others
On the pile
7 other thin brown
Sealed-up
Office envelopes.

Back to bed
To sleep.

   *

Knock, knock.
The door.
I flutter
Back to consciousness.

Knock Knocking –
Knuckles.

Whose?
Not the leg man
I know his knock –
More of a rap

Or the gas man
His is a rappitty tap

Or the milk man –
(He rings the bell)

Knock KNOCK!

I butterfly dive
Back down to the squall
Rubbing my nose
In the sheet-silt
(For comfort)
Holding my foul breath
Hoping the knuckles
Bugger off!

KNOCK! KNOCK!

Those knuckles
Must be skinned!

The penny drops –
I cannonball
Into the vestibule
Drawing a comb
Through my burred locks
Slipping into something see-through
Freshening my breath
By chewing on a brillo-pad

As I squirm-wriggle to the door
And draw back the bolts
I practise my surprise

'Hello?'
(Pink soap suds
Bubble through my teeth)

It isn't him
It isn't the Skin-Shedder

It is a tradesperson
In Corporation green

And waders

Showering raindrops
In thin silver darts
From his shiny black braids

(It's pouring down)

Is it the water-man?

He waves
A
Fish-skin
Bag

It's mine!

'You trapped it'
He says
'In the door
Of a train
Couple of weeks back.

I would have
Brought it back before
But I've been
Draining (temporarily)
The Ancient Lakes

Round Bogota
Recovering
Spanish gold'
(A slug smirks, sceptical?)
'Your address

I found
On your
Crustacean-Enthusiast
Club Card
Inside.'

I swoon – nearly.
Desire bubbles
Pink in me
He has the spirit of a seal
(I feel)

'Come In
Get dry
No, leave the legs there.'

(Dumped by the leg man
Sunday last)

As he watches me
With his black eyes
Slither
To the kitchen

I sense
Like me
He's moist.

*

Dear L.W.
If you should find
My shoes
Could you
Please forward
Them to

New Address
(See Over)

Yours ... S.S.

P.S. Thank you
For a pleasant
Evening.

BRIDGET MEEDS *Light*

To Martin, Jimmy, and Janice

'*Take my hand as the sun descends ...*' Patti Smith

I

At the Big House New Year's Eve karaoke,
two sisters, shiny in cheap black velour,
shout 'Like a. Virgin' into the microphone while their proud da
    beams.
They win second place, and a bottle of wine.
First place and a bottle of spirits goes to the mustachioed fella
who squeaks out a tight-voiced 'Ebony and Ivory'.
The crowd is crazy for him.
The dark-eyed woman beside me hears I'm from New York
and asks if she can stay with me for the World Cup.
Today, the boyfriend came by to tell me he's going back to his
    former girl,
whom he had left for me.
A few minutes past midnight, the New Year comes in with
    bombs,
a dozen fires sprinkled across the city centre.
Here, people jive on the tables.

2

I am working nights illegally in a pizza shop,
where I am paid two quid an hour to answer phones, make pies,
and wait on large drunk men who take the piss out of me
because I say 'tomayto' instead of 'tomahto',
and ask if they can order me on their pie.
I work from half seven till four a.m.
I've been in bed all day, weeping about the boyfriend.
The cook assumes my eyes are red because I'm stoned,
and ribs me for not sharing.
I offer to chop the onions, their juice as thick as milk,
grateful for another chance to cry.
Later, I am out front wiping tables when two RUC Land
    Rovers careen by, sirens breaking,
the sudden flash of blue lights startling and beautiful through
    the steamed front window.

3

The well-fed dogs lie at gates all along Kimberly Street,
or in the middle of the road, or on the faded red, white, and
   blue curbstones.
I realize that these dogs are most likely the ones responsible
for the elaborately curled shit that decorates the gravel-studded
   footpaths,
shit that even the relentless winter rain does not wash away,
but I am nonetheless provoked by their sad eyes to pat their
   sides.
I have just embarrassed myself by going by the boyfriend's
   house,
where he stood in the front garden and told me he couldn't talk
because he had something in the oven,
while the other girl glared at me through the lace curtains.
I am lucky I don't yet know many people in this city,
so I can walk up the road all red and weepy and no one asks
   why.
The Union Jack above the Kimberly Inn hangs limp and wet.
This is a pub where you buzz at the door to be let in, and where,
I've been told, I'd most likely not be welcome, accent and all.

4

After I leave the Dunne's bag on the boyfriend's doorstep,
full of his knickers, tapes, and those D. M. Thomas books he
    gave me,
this flotsam that had been littering the beach of my bedroom,
I buy a green apple and eat it, grateful for the bitterness.
I walk to the city centre, also grateful that the rain has stopped,
and catch the number 61 bus, Carr's Glen via Cavehill,
on my way to a friend who is paying me to type his thesis, titled:
'A Psychological Perspective on Conflict in Northern Ireland'.
The bus groans up the slow slope of Cavehill,
and I watch the outlines of four boys
as they lope along the ridge of the Belfast Waterworks
    Reservoir.
Against this late afternoon sky, they are all black on blue,
just bunchy jackets, short hair, and skinny legs.
The tallest winds up, arm and leg raised,
more beautiful than any baseball player in the States,
and lets the rock fly. I know it's a rock
because it smashes into my window and bounces away,
leaving only a scratch in the Plexiglas.
Later, the British spell-checking program suggests 'jug' as the
    correction for 'Jung',
'intercourse' for 'interchurch', 'Ulcer' for 'Ulster'.

5

It is one a.m. I am typing in my bedroom
and the Chinese woman, who lives next door with her white
    husband and three wee children, is crying.
My pregnant friend has loaned me her manual typewriter, a
    1960 vintage Olympia.
It has no exclamation marks,
so I must assume that strong emotions are a modern invention
and improvise with apostrophe and period.
I have set the typewriter on the rickety metal table
left by the loud, boozy girl who used to have this room,
a girl infamous for seducing a seminarian.
Typing is a noisy matter of bells, thumps, and rattles.
The girls who have lived here for a year and a half
speculate that the Chinese woman is a mail-order bride
and speaks no English. That isn't true, however,
because through the thin wall we share,
I can hear her crying 'I can't, I can't, I can't!'
Her voice spirals higher and higher to a keening, wordless wail.

6

At the Parador, a woman who is buying only lemonades
because she has brought her own bottle in a brown bag
corners me while the barmen glare
and tells me about the time her son was shot;
the time the IRA broke in and held a gun to her head;
and the time her husband went on holiday to America.
He came back with a taste for side salads, fishing trips, and
    dirty movies.
That morning, a note from the boyfriend came in the post
asking me to meet him in Lavery's back bar.
'How are things?' I asked.
'Fine,' he said, his girl was off from school, spending every day
    playing a computer game
while he got stoned and worked on a poem about necrophilia.
I must be getting my sense of humour back, because this made
    me laugh, until I cried,
which provoked him to hold my hand and insist on walking me
    home,
where we stood in front of my gate, kissing in the sleet.
'I'll give you a fucking poem,' says the woman in the Parador,
'write about the fucker in America.'

7

Two weeks after the accidental firebombs, the Linen Hall
    Library is almost back to normal,
the coffee shop open, broken windows replaced, books being
    exchanged once again on trust.
All that remains of the fire are charred sections of shelving
and the lingering scum of soot on the walls.
I've come for *Station Island* but don't stay long.
The boyfriend and I used to meet here for tea and scones,
rubbing knees beneath the glass-topped table.
As I leave, the white-haired security guard
takes a break from checking IDs and tells me they were lucky.
Nearly a thousand biographies were lost,
but the more valuable history collection, much of it
    irreplaceable, was saved.
I suspect biographies are squanders of self-assertion
and these thousand lives are not lost to the world, only Belfast,
but I feel like even mourning them,
the stories of love and politics that have become just the taste of
    ash in my mouth.

7

It's Sunday and raining, and the boyfriend calls by
    unexpectedly.
I invite him in, give him a cup of tea, and we trade stories of
    dreams.
Last night I was a whore, and the night before, a waitress on
    a train.
He's been dreaming of gunfire shattering the bedroom
    windows of their previous apartment,
and those teeth dreams again, his teeth loosening and falling
    out in strange and urgent ways.
Nightmares leave me fatigued, and he seems knackered as
    well.
I look at him and realize I'm already forgetting
the curve of his shoulder in my hand, the taste of his skin.
Last night, I came home from work at five a.m. and ran a hot
    bath.
The bathroom light has been out for six months, so I lay in
    the dark,
soaking the smoke and onion out of my skin.
I've lost nearly a stone since coming to Belfast,
and these surprisingly small hips, girlish belly, and thin thighs
that I soaped and rinsed by feel alone
might belong to another woman for all I can tell.
I soaked and soaked, trying to remember that story about the
    mermaid.
She fell in love, didn't she?
She traded her voice for legs, and, presumably, a crotch.

9

It was bound to happen.
This morning, I went to the laundrette and washed the last
    pieces of clothing he'd peeled off me,
the flowered skirt he'd pulled down over my hips,
the black turtleneck he'd shimmied up over my shoulders and
    head,
the lace bra he'd unclipped with one hand while cupping my
    face with the other.
And the sheets no longer smelled of him either.
I had wakened up a sticky mess of blood. My period was two
    weeks early.
I had to wash them too.
Last night, work was dead slow on account of the rain
that pissed down against the tin kitchen roof and flooded the
    alley.
The cook and I sat in the back, worrying, mopping up the
    muck that seeped under the door.
Tung Sun, the Chinese takeaway down the road,
had been robbed the night before, and he reckoned we were
    next.
Things were so slow, he got to telling me about his girlfriend,
who'd had a miscarriage a few weeks back.
Now all she did was lay around and shout at her kids.
He didn't know what to do.
Fuck's sake, it rained all night and all we did was mop.

10

The IRA launches a mortar attack on the army barracks in
     Crossmaglen,
leaving their van rigged with a second bomb
that explodes when the soldiers drive it in for a closer look.
As we watch the news of 'The Trojan Van',
the girls point out Cross landmarks: it is their hometown.
When we meet people in the pubs, however,
they answer the inevitable 'Where'ya from?'
with 'Near Newry', until they've sussed things out.
I usually answer 'New York', which is true and not true,
since I mean Syracuse and people assume the Bronx,
but the off-key choruses of 'New York, New York'
are easier to endure than the effort of explaining
how two places, the state and the city, share one name,
and one contains the other.

On the single standing wall of a burnt-out house up North
   Queen Street,
a new piece of graffiti has sprouted: 'Greysteel Trick or Treat
   Ha Ha Ha',
signed with a stylized 'UFF'. For a moment I wonder
if this is lit crit of Roddy Doyle, but decide no.
Last night, there was a big scare when the police came on the TV
to warn that Yorkie the tiger had escaped from the zoo
and was roaming North Belfast, hungry and dangerous.
People huddled in their homes, pubs empty,
while army helicopters swept Cavehill with searchlights.
Much later, they thought to drain the moat around the tiger cage
and found Yorkie, heavy and dead and wet.

12

One of the weekend girls took the night off for a piss-up
and came staggering into the shop at half two,
all done up in a short skirt with her hair down,
giggling with her mates and screeching for garlic bread and
    cokes.
Not far behind came the lout she'd just insulted,
who stormed in, called her a cunt, and smashed the radio while
    she hid in the back.
She'd called him a pouf.
'See men!' she shouted after he'd left. She wobbled off towards
    home.
The drivers paced around the kitchen, bouncing on the balls of
    their feet, swinging their arms,
telling well-rehearsed stories of fights.
Later, after we'd closed, I was sweeping when a different fella,
one with a fresh, deepening black eye,
came pounding on the locked door, hungry.
When I shouted that we were closed,
he flipped me off, kicked the window, and limped away down
    the dark street.

13

I ride the fish tank bright bus up the Ormeau Road,
get off at the corner of Ava Avenue, at the Trafalgar Hair
    Studio,
and dodge the thick tea time traffic.
It is half four and already the street lamps flicker red to orange,
the skies deepen from royal blue to black,
the stacked terraced roofs disappear into the night.
The narrow streets echo with the syrupy spring-wound music
of the ice cream truck on its evening rounds,
and the shouts of short-haired boys in gray quilted jackets
who have lit a fire in the front garden of a vacant house.
They slouch around it, sly with pleasure.
The air is hung with thin smoke.
I stop at Michel's and buy clementines, expensive and precious,
    from Spain,
this small, tart fruit necessary for good health,
and peel and eat one as I walk home.
When I dream of him now, he is wearing clothes.
And all of Belfast is bitter with remembered kisses.

In the Big House I meet a man from Dublin who talks at me
   about computers
while he runs his hand up and down my thigh beneath the table.
He insists on giving me his fax number as I leave.
At the party afterwards, I am violently ill,
dead white in the mirror, then mottled and tearsalt streaked
from the compulsive heaving, the cider and bile burning on its
   way up.
Early the next morning, I drag myself from bed and go
   swimming with my pregnant friend.
She appreciates my company during this necessary exercise.
While she paddles lazily, I float in the warm water, aching,
   throat sore,
bleary and estranged in this bright echoing place.
My body is nearly weightless and hardly belongs to me today.
I float and think of his hands on his girl,
she with whom he probably sleeps at this very moment,
hands cupping her bare breasts or spread wide on her belly.
He brought some shade of her body into my bed,
an echo of her pleasure in the ways he touched me,
and sometimes I suspect I know her as intimately as him.
With every sigh and groan I coaxed from him and him from me,
we pulled something else as well,
something we could hardly call love but couldn't name
   otherwise.

15

The boyfriend is driving the borrowed car through Eden,
which is tucked between high-walled Carrickfergus Castle
and Kilroot, the fortress of a power station
that supplies electricity for most of Northern Ireland.
Eden is really just a block of low buildings along the main
     road –
post office, butcher, fruit shop,
and is as cold and grey as the city we've left.
Too clever for my own good, I suggest we stop for apples,
but we are running late, and he doesn't slow the car.
I say 'I feel naked living alone in the city,
I feel like I am missing a limb without you.'
'Not a very important one,' he replies,
distracted by the Land Rover pulling into the lane.

The crack at the shop tonight is all about the Bobbitt acquittal,
which leads the radio news ahead of the bombing in
    Dungannon.
The Irish are really taken with Lorena Bobbitt,
twenty-four-year-old Venezuelan immigrant turned manicurist,
married to a fella so American his name is John Wayne.
He raped her. She cut off his penis and tossed it on a freeway.
She prosecuted for rape and he was found innocent.
He prosecuted for 'malicious wounding' and she was found
    guilty
by reason of insanity, sentenced to time in a mental hospital.
In the meantime, she's posing for *Playboy*, a sex symbol.
The drivers are on about it, not convinced that you can rape the
    wife.
I don't argue, I just carry the big yellow-handled knife around,
    swiping playfully as they go by.
'I'd call that cow a cunt,' says one, 'but that's a useful thing.'

The pool today is full of rude wee boys who shout and splash,
not caring whom they souse with their spray.
My pregnant friend and I finish our laps early to avoid them.
There are workmen in the women's changing room, so we
    must change instead in the men's.
We are suddenly shy in the open showers, used to the discrete
    stalls for women.
We strip off our skin-tight suits and wash ourselves, thighs
    and bellies blue-veined from the cold,
hers large, round, and firm; mine flat.
We pad barefoot to the lockers, our bodies glistening with wet,
water running from our long hair in streams.
We dry ourselves with rough towels – first the hair, face, and
    arms,
then the breasts, back, legs, and feet.
We are tired, lethargic, slow from the weight of the body
    finding itself once again on land.
We dress and only then resume talking, smiling shyly,
    clothed.

18

The boyfriend and I go to see the exhibit by the German
    artist.
The main attraction is four giant spools, tall as me,
perhaps originally for electrical cable but now fitted with
    metal punctured in swirls.
They are placed mathematically across the black plastic floor,
each trailed by a path of white sand
as if it had sifted from the spool as it rolled.
The title translates as 'The Landscape of Mental Confusion',
and the boyfriend examines the sculpture closely.
He crouches and squints. 'It's fake,' he concludes,
'he didn't really roll these across the floor. He sifted the sand
    by hand.'
He touches his finger to it and leaves a single, deep print.
For a moment I feared he was going to write his name.
Later, over a pint, he says, 'I think you are the most
    dishonest person I know.'
We are talking about writing.
He is not aware that he is becoming more of a character than
    a lover to me.
He buys me a gin and bitter lemon. He asks if he can call by
    the next day.
He goes home to his girl.
It is strange to be happy about any of this.

Before *Brookside*, I watch the UTV report of the kneecapping
   at the Hatfield on Saturday night.
There's footage of the fella all doped up on morphine.
Although he is naked but for his underpants as he sprawls on
   the hospital bed,
and the camera lingers lovingly on the stained gauze
round his knees and ankles, on his black and swollen toes,
on his eyes dilated and calm, this is no sexual pose.
Then there's footage of his mum, a woman with cried-out eyes,
who recites a catalogue of dead or wounded brothers, husband,
   and sons.
And her this whole life living on the Lower Ormeau.
Sitting on the settee in the unearthly light of the TV,
I consider the verbs we have made from body parts:
to eye, to face, to foot, to shoulder, to back, to arm.

20

A Catholic man was shot by the UFF last night
in a house on Candahar Street, four blocks from mine.
It was noted as the first sectarian killing of the year.
As I settled deeper under my duvet, half-reading, half-asleep,
someone, I speculate, was drumming his fingers on a
    dashboard
and jiggling a gun against his knee. As I turned off the big
    light,
the sledgehammer must have hit the door, a woman screamed,
feet thudded upstairs and down again. I fell asleep before the
    sirens began,
and dreamed of the fire barn a block away from my
    childhood home.
My brothers and I learned to decode the combinations of
    long and short horn blasts
that signified the different types of fires for the neighborhood
    volunteers,
who would roar up the street towards the station in response,
and we each developed uncanny and annoying siren shrieks
that we would unleash on each other when too excited to sleep.
The wailing, once proved groundless, would provoke my
    harried mother to tears.
The first night the girls heard me typing, they thought it was
    gunshots,
but were too knackered to leave bed and investigate.
Certainly this borrowed British typewriter that squats on my
    table is no gun.

21

12" ham papple 28 St Jude's Pd; 8" mr pponi 1 grlc bd 4
Rosetta Pk; 15" tuna scorn xchs 12 Univ Ave.
One of the drivers gets tipped with some blow and we take
turns in the alley, getting stoned.
12" ham 2 dcoke 4 Deramore Ave; 15" ½ sal ½ pponi 25
Annadale Crescent; 12" onion ppr pponi 14 Gipsy St.
A three-legged dog hops in through the open door and stands
at the counter, earnest and expectant.
2 grlc bd sprme 4 lemon fanta 5 S Parade; 8" xchs grlc olive 4
My Lady's Rd; 15" tuna banana 11 Ava Pk.
It is cold when we arrive but warmer when we leave. The
sky is considering the eventuality of light.

22

The boyfriend is driving without his seatbelt when the police
   pull us over.
The RUC man, blond and burly with the glamour of his thick
   flak jacket and high-brimmed cap,
smiles and fires questions as his partner taps the bonnet with the
   tip of a boxy gun.
'Is this your licence, son? What's your date of birth? Why
   doesn't this photo look like you? Is this your car? Whose car
   is it? What's your date of birth? What's your address?
   Whereabouts is that? Are you a student? Is this your car?
   What's your date of birth? Where are you coming from?
   Where are you going?'
He writes the information down in his black-bound book and
   lets us go with a warning.
We get on with going where we're going.
The wheelie-bins gather at the mouths of alleys: full,
   penitential, silent.

23

The girls and I go for a Sunday afternoon ramble in the
 Belvoir Park Forest,
now a National Trust Park, but once, a large estate, and
 before that,
an outpost of seventeenth-century Anglo-Norman invaders.
Near the entrance, we climb the motte,
a flat-topped hill built by them as a lookout post.
Grown over with brush and long, brown grass,
it is twenty feet high and thirty across,
and true, from the top you can see the Lagan looping around
 this small valley.
It shines in the lowering sun.
We clamber down and continue walking, off the tarmac onto
 the dirt path,
a wet narrow tunnel through laurel and ivy.
The muck sucks at our boots, thick obscene goo, chocolate-
 coloured and smelling of rot.
But it's not completely winter: grass is beginning to grow,
and urgent shoots of snowdrops and daffodils cluster beneath
 the weeping ash,
those old mossy trees embossed with carvings: 'UDA 1975',
 'UFF POLVFB', 'UVF 1983'.
We are far now from the brightly dressed families that clotted
 the paved path.
It gets dark. We realize we're lost.

24

I have the cold on me, all drip and cough,
and I've been having more nightmares, complete with the
   sweats and rigid shakes.
This morning I awoke from one in which everyday objects – a
   hairbrush, a tin of beans –
became threatening in the hands of my mother.
A letter from her had arrived in the post. She wrote mostly of
   the weather, saying
'The boys had to shovel the snow off the roof and chip the ice.
We've had about 88 inches of snow and the ice was backing up
   and coming in.
It's been a raw winter. The snow is so deep. The banks are four
   feet high.'
This afternoon, the boyfriend and I ducked into Morrison's to
   avoid a sudden sleet shower,
which he insisted on calling snow.
We made a strange sight among the suited businessmen
in our DMs, tatty jackets, and unwashed hair.
He told me he's decided there's no reason to write poetry.
Despite everything, we still sat with our thighs touching,
and when I, drunk, began to cry about my grown brothers stuck
   at home with our sick mother, he took my hand.
You'd have to write a novel to explain this mess.
No doubt I will. No doubt he won't.

25

Last night, gale force twelve winds and a rough sea battered
    the coast.
The salt in the wind-blown spray coated the insulators at the
    Kilroot power station,
which tripped the system. The Ballylumford backup failed,
and a power cut plunged seventy per cent of Northern Ireland
    into sudden dark.
My Irish teacher was driving me home from a class on
    Islandmagee.
As the car shook in the wind, he taught me the possessive
    pronouns,
and I repeated after him: 'mo, do, a, a, ar, bhur, a.'
We wound slowly along the narrow coast road, avoiding
    downed branches and clumps of gorse.
He began to explain the past tense, but it was too
    complicated
and by then we were in Belfast anyway,
where the driving, without light or traffic signals,
was much more difficult. Our minds were on the road.
We coasted through intersections, fingers crossed.

26

Secretly I'd love another go at the boyfriend,
one nose-crunching blow to put me at the forefront of his
    mind again.
I've only hurt him physically twice before,
the first a smack with the flat of my open hand on his back
that night he called me her name instead of mine.
We sprang apart and crouched on opposite sides of the bed,
panting with anger like cats.
That was our first argument: how I could I hit him, he spat,
he who would never so much as raise his voice to me?
I refused to debate, snarling with fury.
The second time was the next night, when he asked me to
    choke him,
and I did, and he seemed to enjoy it. But that was that, no more.
Later, when he left me, he said
'God, it'd be easier if you'd just hit me instead of crying,'
but of course it was different, once again.
I didn't want to hit him then. Why now?
I wake from dreams of the stranger he's chosen to be, furious
    and sweating, hands clenched.
It's like when I was a child and would go rigid with anger at
    my brothers
for inconsequential slights. I would hit them as long as I could,
as hard as I could, until my always astonished mother pulled
    me away.
I don't understand. I must be learning something from all this.
I think I have to tell myself that.

At the GAA social club in Claudy,
the old men lean into the corners, chain-smoking,
talking quietly and fluently in Irish.
My teacher darts from table to table, handing out sheets for the
    quiz.
He has invited me here, hoping to improve my accent.
I am shy, bewildered by the streams of sound.
You can't step in the same river twice,
and if I stop concentrating for even a moment, I am lost.
I am obviously the only stranger in this small hall,
and the men stare. I try not to stare back,
smiling in an attempt to look friendly.
Most likely I just look daft.
Soon, a man drifts away from his group to me
and says 'Dia duit.' 'Dia s' Muire duit,' I reply.
With his prompting, I manage a stammered, brave
'Brid an t-ainm ata orm, agus ta me i mo chonai i mBeal feirste.'
My teacher, eyes glinting, swoops by and murmurs 'Ta si
    American.'
The man smiles and nods, and returns to his table.
I understand little of the quiz, just the questions about films,
and find myself laughing with the crowd at the jokes I don't
    understand,
just to keep from feeling lonely.
Afterwards, the women appear with trays of buns and tea.
'Go raibh maith agat,' I say. 'Oh, thank you.'
I am tired but my teacher needs to stay a bit longer,

his hand on my shoulder as he talks energetically in this
     language I barely understand
to men who shift from foot to foot and look at me shyly
     beneath their eyelashes.
At last we go, and he speeds all the way.
We fly over the Bann, up and over the Glenshane Pass,
and out to the coast, towards what I catch myself calling home.

The landlord came by and fixed the bathroom light,
which had been out for nearly eight months.
The girls and I went to the pub to celebrate,
and we didn't realize until we stumbled home
that he had fixed it so well, it wouldn't switch off.
After the dark, we face eternal light.
Though we worry about the electric bill,
it's not so bad — we can see so much more.
I can actually see myself in the mirror, unshadowed,
drunk and puffy, or beautiful, or tired.
I can see how long my hair has grown,
and the uncertain color of my eyes,
which, the boyfriend used to tell me,
change depending on my mood.
I hadn't known that, and didn't quite believe him.
Now I can see for myself.

29

The knives at work are increasingly dull,
though still sharp enough to cut flesh,
as I demonstrate by slicing off the top of my left thumb
for the second time in a month.
The first time, I was in a hurry, whacking at pepperoni
with customers lined to the door, when the knife slipped
and I hinged a flap of skin across the tip.
I bled a brilliant red through a twist of apron,
making one-handed, misshapen pies.
It healed to a curious sunken circle of scab,
an interruption in the sleek, unique whorl of thumbprint.
Last night, I managed to cut it again,
while chopping onions during the after-pub rush.
This time, however, there was no blood –
just a dark, red line gouged into the scar tissue,
a groove in the thickening skin.
Ach, there's no reason to whinge.
The papery sting of a cut on my thumb is not going to kill me.

I can't shake this cold, and wake with a fever.
My skin hurts, dry with heat, and I ache.
In the afternoon, I wander to Bishop's for tea and chips
but run into the boyfriend by the Crescent,
who suggests a hot whiskey as cure.
He is a follower of the 'feed a fever' theory.
I agree, and the first leads to another, and another,
and it's true, I do eventually feel better, or at least different,
because then it's dark already, has been for a while,
and he's walking me to the taxi stand,
arm slung over my shoulder carelessly,
and while we wait we kiss once, fiercely,
and then he holds my hand in both of his,
hanging his head, his hair in his face.
I go home alone and wake very early,
sweating and weeping, covers flung to the floor.
I think my fever's broke. I watch the sky lighten.
For the first time, I feel guilty.
It is Valentine's Day, and the only real snow of the year,
a blizzard of an inch that shuts down the city.
Across the doorsteps of West Belfast,
the UFF leaves bombs concealed in heart-shaped boxes of
   chocolates.

31

The seventeenth-century rocking horse is in a state of half-
   repair,
resting quietly on its thin rockers in the middle of the antique
   market
in the church hall on Donegal Pass.
I am looking for a gift for my friend's unborn baby.
The nap of the horse's skin is worn nearly away from around
   the haunches and head,
and the tiny leather harness, looped between tarnished brass
   hoops, is cracked.
But someone has sewn in a new coarse rope mane and tail,
and repainted the wood block hooves and mouth.
It seems clumsy to restore something so old.
While more realistic than its modern relative,
with legs that taper delicately, painted teeth, and scratched
   button eyes,
it is still stiff and out of proportion, head too big for the body.
If a child of today, large from vitamins and good bread,
rode it with inattentive vigor,
no doubt it would crack off the rockers, the spindly legs
   splinter,
the bit would come off in the hand. It is no longer the toy it
   was,
though people pause at it, saying the names of children
   hopefully.
'Matthew ... ,' says a man.
'Yes,' replies a woman, 'it'd be good for him.'

But they walk on. It is much too costly, and obviously not for
    children at all.
A rocking horse is a toy you remember all your life,
but eventually as a frustrating plaything –
all that riding, only to dismount in the place you left.
I am beginning to think that my friend's baby would be better
    off without one.
I leave the horse there, motionless amidst the paintings of
    church elders and the mirrors flaking silver,
with only its clouded reflection for comfort.

Where I come from, Orangemen are basketball players for
  Syracuse University.
Blue and orange are their school colours,
and their mascot is a giant stuffed orange with eyes and little
  blue arms and legs.
The mascot used to be the 'Saltine Warrior',
an Indian with a savage grimace and orange feather head-dress.
Saltine referred to the now defunct salt mines on which
  Syracuse long ago was built.
But in the early 80s, the local Onondaga tribe complained,
tired of the fake war whoops that echoed from the Manley
  Field House over to the reservation.
A marketing consultant was employed and, after research,
designed the 'Orange', meant to be a positive image with
  which the crowds would be pleased to identify.
It seems to have worked a charm, because the team soon hit
  the big time.
The Carrier Dome, with more seating and amenities, was built,
and they began to win game after game. My brothers and I
  were big fans,
and I had my first crushes on those ball-wielding demigods.
There was Matt Roe, so tall, short-haired as a soldier,
and of course Dwayne 'The Pearl' Washington,
whose superhuman basket, lobbed from half-court at the
  buzzer,
won us the NCAA Big East championship over St John's.
The team displayed grace and skill that endures in my memory,
despite later drug and legal problems when players went pro.

His girl's mother took sick so she went home.
He and I got stupid drunk and fell back into bed.
It can't have been all that romantic:
he hadn't a bath in days, and I was still full up from this cold
that has lingered for weeks, blurry, stuffy, dripping with snot.
He came but I couldn't,
and I woke us throughout the night with my cough,
that deep, persistent, and painful reflex.
In the morning, he made me a hot honey and lemon,
and after I drank the thick, almost-sweet drink,
I lay with my head in his lap, like a child or an animal.
He held my hand and stroked my hair.
'This doesn't change anything,' he said. 'I'm not going to
     leave her.'
'OK,' I said, 'but I'm still not keeping any secrets for you.'

The streets of Belfast are paved with broken glass.
I'm like a magpie, my eye caught
by the green glitter of bits of bottle in gravel,
the hunks of shattered mirrors around skips,
the bright sprinkle in mud of emptied window panes.
This morning I noticed that an entire bus shelter panel had been
    smashed –
one of those annoying ones with the daft margarine advert:
'If I love you then I need you,
if I need you then I want you around.'
What that has to do with fake butter, I don't know.
In any case, it was thick glass,
specially made with this sort of violence in mind,
because instead of breaking into long, sharp daggers,
it crumbled into countless round-edged kernels
that lay in heaps on the sidewalk, blue as ice.
They could have been jewels or teeth,
and a few larger pieces, crazed with cracks,
were still wedged into the corners of the frame.
The boyfriend once told me that the sound of glass breaking
the second after a bomb blast in the city centre
was beautiful. It's amazing, so it is,
how they've designed glass that sounds beautiful in the
    breaking
but isn't dangerous when broken.
I can pick up bits, put them in my pocket, and safely take them
    home.

35

This afternoon, I watch *SuperTed* on Children's BBC.
This muscular cartoon bear is no normal toy;
no, he is a bear in possession of extra-ursine powers
including speech, flight, and rational thought.
Today he is on holiday on the coast of North Wales.
He has little time to enjoy himself, however.
Soon SuperTed finds himself, as you do,
on the trail of evil gun-running pirates led by Tex,
a Captain Hook look-a-like with an American accent.
While bringing the guns to shore,
the bumbling pirates have captured a buxom Welsh farm girl
and threaten her with impure intentions.
But have no fear, wee viewers!
One particularly foolish pirate mistakes a hand grenade
for a piece of fruit, and bites it.
It explodes, and his bellowing alerts SuperTed
to the location of their cavern hideout.
Our spandex-clad hero flies in, punches Tex, and saves the girl.
All is well. They sit on the beach and eat biscuits.
Now it is time for *Oprah*, and later, the news.

This March sun is sexy and shy,
first full with an almost tangible weight,
then hiding coyly beneath an edge of cloud,
and out again, sliding long fingers across my walls.
There is a tinge of warmth in the air. I open my coat.
I have been to the clinic for medicine,
and my cold, which had turned to infection, seems finally to
    be easing.
My ears have popped, the lessened pressure and clearer sound
something I didn't even know I had missed.
This morning I got my period,
felt thankful for the deep ache and welcome red,
and I posted a letter of vague apology to his girl.
The snowdrops that struggled through the hard ground of the
    garden are opening,
and I couldn't give a fuck.

37

When my older brother enlisted in the army three days after
    high school graduation,
he was first sent to boot camp in Fort Leonard Wood, Missouri,
where he had his head shaved, lost forty pounds, and
    acquired a Southern accent.
He was next stationed in Fort Bragg, North Carolina,
where he took up smoking and drinking whiskey neat.
There, his accent grew stronger, his vowels sprawling across
    rooms
and infuriating me. It seemed false, and even worse,
a betrayal: every exaggerated 'Shi-i-i-t' and 'Y'all'
took him farther away from us all.
This was during the time when Mom was getting sicker
and it must have been strange for him to see her change so
    drastically on each visit,
her increasing gauntness not so apparent to us who saw her
    each day.
We all lost perspective that year.
'Y'all don't seem to be takin' good care of Ma,'
he said once, swirling the whiskey in his glass.
'Mom is fine,' I snapped, sixteen and judgmental and tired.
Still, I did his wash for him on those visits, fuming among his
    graying socks
while he dissolved everyone upstairs to tears with stories
    about his good ol' boys,
stories somehow funnier in his new drawl.
Now I am the one far away from home and our still-sick Mom,
more 'achs' and 'ayes' peppering my speech every day.

Yesterday at work I heard myself say
'Ach, you wouldn't give us the brush?'
when I meant 'Please hand me the broom.'

38

When we were together, he would often get me stoned,
and we would sink into bed and drift away the day.
And when I later couldn't sleep, he would hold me
and make up fairy tales about people we knew.
'I'll stay awake until you sleep,' he would promise, and he
    would.
In the morning, we never wanted to get up.
I still don't sleep well, and at first, newly alone in my narrow
    bed,
I'd lie in the dark for hours, not thinking much
but listening to the honk of the occasional taxi (in which he
    never came)
and watching the slashes of street light sway on my wall
as the blind drifted in the draft.
Later, I gave that up, and now when I can't sleep,
I just flood the room with the big light
and read, write letters home, watch the sun rise.

39

My mother has been afraid of water since she was twelve,
when she fell off a dock into Owasco Lake.
Her long hair and heavy wool skirt welcomed the water and
    dragged her down,
and all she remembers is a faraway voice calling her name;
her mother's face, distorted through the lens of water;
and a hand, becoming clear as it broke through the surface.
    Then black.
She must have been saved, because she became my mother,
who never swam, wore slacks, and always had short hair.
I remembered this story tonight as I lay in the bath, my hair
    floating around me as I soaked.
It is the longest I've ever grown it; it reaches past my shoulder
    blades when I stand.
I surprise myself with this girl I now see in the mirror.
Most of my life, I've kept it boy-short,
a habit left over from when our Saturday night excitement
was Mom cutting our hair, with a bowl as guide.
After she stopped, I still kept it short, but my Saturday nights
    became different,
a time when I would leave them all watching TV and steal
    away to the bathroom for a long soak,
where I told myself complicated stories in which I was always
    the heroine,
strong and smart, but also beautiful.
It was one of those nights that I must have first touched
    myself
and been surprised with a shy shudder of response.

Tonight, clean, I touched myself for the first time since he left
    me,
right hand moving slow and then fast, left tenderly cupping a
    breast,
welcoming myself once again to this world.

To get to the newspaper room at the Belfast Central Library,
I must first apply to the librarian,
who gives me the once-over twice and grudgingly agrees.
She leads me round the desk, into the back,
and marches me through the dim maze of the stacks,
her heels a fusillade of clicks on the tile.
She shoves at the wonky lift door with an irritated grunt
I think she suspects my accent or disapproves of my short skirt,
or perhaps it is merely impatience with the slow descent
which provokes her to cross her arms and tap her foot.
Once in the sanctum of the newspaper room,
I am instructed to sign my name and address
and am handed into the care of a laconic young man
who fetches the heavy bound volume I need.
I am the only reader here.
The grey metal shelves stretch away into dark,
piled with the long, moribund books that smell so invitingly of
    dust
and are full of years of Belfast news, now out-of-date.
But these old records of election results and wedding notices
are valued enough to be kept safe here,
tended by this keeper who reminds me to turn the fragile pages
    with care.
Rows of fluorescent lights line the ceiling, though only the ones
    over the desks are lit.
I read what I came for. The librarian leads me back a different
    way

and lets me out a door onto a street I have never seen before. I start walking, sure I'll eventually know where I am, and am right.

The boyfriend's been away for a few days
and asks me to meet him at Lavery's on his return.
He drinks pints of cider and black, but I'm on the Ballygowan,
still on antibiotics, grumpy and cautious of my health.
We discuss the recent tragic excesses of Kurt Cobain,
and disagree: I find him more annoying than profound.
I suggest we go and look at the new gallery exhibit,
but he claims they close early at the weekend.
Still, I don't have the money or inclination to spend my whole
    afternoon in the pub,
so I get up to go. As I shrug on my coat,
he runs his hand down the back of my thigh and cups the curve
    of my calf.
My stomach lurches at his touch.
He stares into his pint.
I'd be lying if I said I was over him,
and I don't want to be.
Nonetheless, I leave, and I leave him there.

42

I first noticed the difference between Hiberno- and American-
  English
in the way people pronounced the word 'now'.
Here, I hear everything from 'nigh' to 'nahr' to 'nowr',
but never the 'now' I know. And it is more important,
an imperative heaved lovingly into every command.
The Irish for 'now' is 'anois',
which I am tempted to hear as 'anise',
whose licorice-flavoured seeds are used in cordials,
or 'a niche', meaning a space or welcomed recess.
Forgive my sin of understanding one language
through its unmeant echoes in another.
Look at it this way: the 'one' in 'one language'
can be heard as 'won', which is 'now' spelled backwards,
and is the state of a gift given freely and received by chance.

43

I come home at four a.m., take a bath, and go to sleep.
All of what I call night, I dream of making pizzas,
the most perfect I've ever made, one after another,
round, symmetrical, cooked exactly the right length of time.
I am happy, singing along with the radio,
the oven shovel and cutter as natural to me as my hands and
    arms.
I wake to a cold, clear afternoon. It is the last day of winter.
I sit around for a while, gossiping with the girls,
then dress and line my eyes with kohl, carefully.
I'm on again at half four. As I walk up the road,
the daffodils ripple in waves across the Ormeau Park, in full-
    bloom.
I am surprised to find the owner's brother-in-law painting the
    shop – the health inspector is due.
He is just finishing, wiping drips and washing brushes,
and then he sits and smokes, muttering about the wife.
He asks me what I think, and I tell him:
he's done a lovely job. The place looks almost different.
After he leaves, I make up a batch of dough and knead it,
the balls soft and warm as breasts in my hands.
I take my time. I've hours before the sun sets,
and the rush begins once again.

Belfast, Winter 1994